SOCIOLOGY

SOCIOLOGY
A Seventh-day Adventist Approach
for Students and Teachers

Lionel Matthews

ANDREWS
UNIVERSITY PRESS

BERRIEN SPRINGS, MICHIGAN

Andrews University Press
Sutherland House
Berrien Springs, MI 49104-1700 U.S.A.
Telephone: 269-471-6134
Fax: 269-471-6224
Email: aupo@andrews.edu
Website: http://universitypress.andrews.edu

ISBN 978-1-883925-55-0
Library of Congress Control Number: 2006932172

Printed in the United States of America
10 09 08 07 06   5 4 3 2 1

Scriptural quotations are taken from the King James Version.

Editing   Kevin Wiley, Tara Marion
Cover Design   Christopher Peteranecz

Publication of this book has been sponsored by:

The Institute for Christian Teaching
General Conference Education Department
12501 Old Columbia Pike
Silver Spring, MD 20904-6600, U.S.A.
Telephone: (301) 680-5060
Fax: (301) 622-9627
Website: http://ict.adventist.org
Email: rodrigueze@gc.adventist.org

The Center for College Faith
Andrews University
Berrien Springs, MI 49104 U.S.A.
Telephone: (269) 471-6291
Email: kutzner@andrews.edu

TABLE OF CONTENTS

ABOUT THIS BOOK AND SERIES

This volume is one of an ongoing series about integrating faith with learning. The series is being co-sponsored by the Institute for Christian Teaching (ICT) at the Education Department of the General Conference of Seventh-day Adventists and the Center for College Faith (CCF) at Andrews University. While the present work concerns the teaching of sociology, two previously published volumes have dealt with the teaching of history and the teaching of literature in an Adventist setting. Future books are anticipated.

All teaching in Seventh-day Adventist institutions has an overriding goal of building faith not only in the Christian message but also in the Adventist understanding of Christianity and in its mission to the world. However, Adventist schools teach a broad range of subject matter, much of which is generally thought of as secular. The Adventist teacher of sociology must use a textbook that is written by scholars who are not necessarily believers and who might even be hostile to religion. The instructor must deal with material that on the surface does not appear to have spiritual value. How then can Adventist teachers of sociology (or any other discipline) build faith in the essentials of Christianity and Adventism while at the same time covering the material essential for an understanding of the discipline?

This volume addresses that challenge. It is not intended to be a textbook in sociology. The author does not attempt to plumb its various sub-divisions. Rather it is a supplement to which teachers and students can turn for insights about how to weave faith into their study of sociology. It holds that all truth is God's truth if only with the eye of faith we can see beneath the surface of the apparently secular and discern that God is working there also.

While the book is primarily intended for use by teachers and students pursuing sociology in Adventist institutions of higher learning, it might also prove useful for students studying sociology at non-Adventist colleges and universities. It is vital that these students emerge from their programs of study with heightened faith and a driving sense of mission for God and His world. It is with this hope and prayer that we publish this third volume in the series.

THE CENTER FOR COLLEGE FAITH BOARD

FOREWORD

Sociology: A Seventh-day Adventist Approach for Students and Teachers is the third book in a "how to" series that is designed to build a library of knowledge relating academic disciplinary topics to issues of faith. The integration of faith and learning is a concept long held as an essential part of the educational focus of the Seventh-day Adventist Church. Thus, in conjunction with the Center for College Faith at Andrews University, the General Conference Education Department has attempted to foster the perspective that committed Christian teachers must develop a way to blend biblical faith perspectives with intellectual concepts. In the current book, *Sociology*, Lionel Matthews attempts to do just that by suggesting an approach to the infusion of sociological concepts into a faith perspective.

The Bible is replete with examples of the importance of relationships—with God, with human beings, among God's people, and between God's people and others who do not know God and His ways. Given the various cultural milieus in which Seventh-day Adventists live and work throughout the world, the topics that sociology addresses appear to have a natural connection. Yet seldom has the Church considered the intellectual contribution that the discipline can provide as part of a worldview into the life of the Christian.

Sociologists view the world from three main theoretical perspectives. These perspectives are the lens through which behavior is studied and understood. The *functionalist* perspective focuses on the way parts of society—such as the family, religion, and government—contribute to the stability of the entire social system. The *conflict* perspective focuses on the social processes of tension, competition, and change, whereas the *interactionist* perspective focuses on the way people act toward, respond to, and influence one another. These perspectives provide a good starting point for a dialogue about helping people form a connection between theory and real life.

Culture, roles and statuses, and interaction between people and people groups, between societies, and between large and small groups are the fertile field which forms the background for the idea of this volume. Viewing the Bible through the lens that Matthews provides offers one the opportunity to ask different questions regarding commonly accepted events of Scripture. In biblical times as well as today, wherever there are different roles and statuses in a society, where some people are treated as superiors and others as subordinates, and where other instances of social inequality exist, these speak to a sociological perspective. This book opens a vista into our thinking on some of these topics.

Thus, *Sociology: A Seventh-day Adventist Approach for Students and Teachers* not only speaks to issues that help one integrate faith into practical Christian life, but it also provides a larger window into a world of ideas that take on world perspectives—conflict, confluence, postmodernism, and the like. The subject matter in this volume is long overdue, and while the author does not attempt to offer the book as a major sociological treatise, the perspective he shares does add to the fertile field of how to integrate faith perspectives into the teaching of sociological concepts. This is a major contribution to the growing literature on the topic of the integration of faith and learning.

C. Garland Dulan
Director, Department of Education
General Conference of Seventh-day Adventists

PREFACE

Christian educational institutions engage the ongoing challenge of making every subject that comprises the teaching curriculum a means through which wholeness in Christ can be facilitated. Hence, the struggle has always been one of finding points of convergence between disciplines such as sociology, which embrace the canon of science as proof, and a faith perspective that does not necessarily appeal to such a source of legitimation.

In the chapters that follow, I have sought to identify linkages between sociology and Christianity with a view of demonstrating that the two can be integrated. Specifically, it has been my aim to show the relevance of sociology to the Seventh-day Adventist worldview and to depict ways by which the study and teaching of this discipline can facilitate greater clarity and understanding of this denomination's worldview. This task I have attempted in six chapters.

In Chapter One, I discuss three reasons why Christians should study sociology. These include the biblically-based group focus of the discipline, its potential to instill in people an awareness of themselves and others, and its capacity to empower people with a thorough grasp of their cosmos.

In Chapter Two, I examine the sociological perspective in some detail. Here I trace the development of the discipline, focusing upon its philosophical and theoretical underpinnings. In the process, the divergent as well as the convergent strands of sociology and religion are underscored and discussed.

In Chapter Three, I discuss the Seventh-day Adventist Church as a product of divine intervention as well as social conditioning. With respect to the latter, I trace evidence back to the doctrinal and structural development of Seventh-day Adventism over time.

In Chapter Four, I explore the definition of the faith/learning integration construct in order to indicate ways by which integration may take place between faith and learning in sociology.

In Chapter Five, I highlight the value of perspectives, specifically focusing upon how, through the teaching and study of sociology, elements of the twenty-eight fundamentals of Adventism may be better communicated and understood.

In Chapter Six, I briefly examine the challenges that modernism and postmodernism pose to the faith/discipline integration. The section that follows Chapter Six presents valuable bibliographic sources for those who wish to pursue an interest in sociology as a faith-supportive discipline.

Acknowledgments

I truly believe that that which we often deem our personal achievement is far more embedded in the social and the spiritual than we are willing to concede. In this regard, I concur with Perdue (1986) that "…even the master [the author] is more a medium than creator" (p. xiii). It is in this spirit that I acknowledge my enormous debt to all those (past and present) from whom I have drawn insights, received encouragement, and have otherwise been sustained in this task. The list of those to whom gratitude is due can therefore be interminable, but I must single out a few persons for special mention.

First, my gratitude to the Center for College Faith, Andrews University, and the General Conference Department of Education for providing me with the opportunity to write this volume. In particular, Humberto Rasi and Gary Ross must be acknowledged for the personal interest they showed in the formative stages of the project. My gratitude to Ken Crane, Harold James, Delmer Davis, and Roger Dudley, each of whom has read the entire manuscript and offered useful comments. Roger Dudley was especially helpful in the revisions that ensued upon the peer review process and must know how grateful I am. Gary Land and Duane McBride have been enduring in their encouragements and comments. Duane McBride stands out not only in his encouragement but also for his informed advocacy of the project. I would especially like to thank Bruce Closser for his editorial expertise and advice, as well as the editorial staff of Andrews University Press. For the comments and suggestions of the various peer reviewers, I am deeply appreciative and grateful. Colwick Wilson, Elvin Gabriel, and Hilton Garnett deserve special mention. While Colwick Wilson was often my late-night sounding board, the latter two were a constant support. My former reader, Derek Bacchus; my son, Jermey; and my wife, Walterine, must be thanked for their unwavering willingness to type and retype the often hard-to-decipher manuscript. Not to forget my caring daughters, Jermella and Jonelle, who allowed me the space, sometimes in the wee hours of the morning away from home, to undertake this task. My gratitude to them.

Finally, to God be the glory for His all-sustaining and empowering grace.

Lionel Matthews
Department of Behavioral Sciences
Andrews University
Berrien Springs, MI 49104 U.S.A.
matthews@andrews.edu

References

Perdue, W. D. (1986). *Sociological theory: Explanation, paradigm, and ideology.* Palo Alto, CA: Mayfield Publishing Company.

CHAPTER ONE

WHY CHRISTIANS SHOULD STUDY SOCIOLOGY

This chapter acknowledges misconceptions associated with sociology and discusses the reason for the inclusion of sociology as part of a balanced curriculum. Three reasons are then advanced as to why Christians ought to study sociology. These include the biblically-based group focus of the discipline, its potential to instill in people an awareness of themselves and others, and its capacity to empower people with a thorough grasp of their social world.

Some Christians, Perkins (1987) has observed, have "deep misgivings about sociology." The fear is that students who take sociology as a course in college may have their religious conviction "...undermined, if not destroyed" (p. 13). However, in spite of the alleged fear,[1] Christian colleges and universities continue to offer sociology as a course to their students. In light of this, it seems relevant to ask the following questions: Why do professors and students at Christian colleges teach and study sociology? Can the teaching and study of sociology facilitate a deeper understanding of the Christian life? Can it serve as a vehicle for building faith?

To begin to understand the reason for offering sociology as an academic discipline at a Christian college/university, we must first understand the broader purpose of the educational enterprise. Educational institutions aim at exposing students to a variety of experiences, with the ultimate purpose of preparing them for life. The goal of the education offered, at least from the Christian standpoint, is to equip students with the knowledge, skills, dispositions, and perspectives that will enable them to live meaningfully and fully in this world as a preparation for heaven. Hence, the selection of a curriculum for a Christian school presupposes a careful analysis and grasp of humans' life activities and need dispositions. Thus questions are raised as to how these life activities and need dispositions

---

1. The social construction focus of the discipline, the view that reality is basically a human-made product, seems to be the source of concern for some, and the basis of the perceived threat. (See Chapter 2 for a more detailed discussion.)

are to be characterized, and what, in this light, constitutes a meaningful educative process.

Though positions vary on the qualities that are considered central to a person's development, and those deemed important but not central (Pring, 1987), educators generally agree on the holistic nature of human beings. Despite the varied views advanced on this subject (Nohria, Lawrence, & Wilson, 2001; Ryan & Deci, 2000; Thompson, Grace, & Cohen, 2001), some basic needs have been determined. Maslow (1970) conceives of these in terms of lower and higher order needs. He identifies six levels of need, with the physiological being the lowest and self-actualization the highest. Pratt's (1994) classification of philosophical, social, aesthetic, and survival needs is similar to Ellen White's (1903) formulation of the physical, mental, spiritual, and social faculties. Based on these categorized needs, core experiences considered necessary to facilitate a person's meaningful and optimum development have been identified.

Educational institutions, particularly Christian schools, aim at providing a balanced education. Thus, the various core areas of the curriculum—such as the natural sciences, the social sciences, the arts, and the humanities—take a cue from and are organized in keeping with the needs identified above. The objective is to facilitate the individual students' optimal development in the way best suited to these needs. As White (1903) has suggested, the process of education is concerned with the holistic development of the mental, physical, spiritual, and moral faculties, with the ultimate goal being the Godlikeness of the student. In this regard, where does sociology come in?

The Sociological Focus

Sociology, like the other social sciences (psychology, anthropology, political science, and economics), is concerned with the study of human behavior. Why, then, should not any one of these disciplines suffice for an understanding of the social dimension of human life? The reason lies in the complex nature of human beings, which cannot be understood from a single perspective, and in the efforts of various scholars to understand the human condition from their various philosophical positions.

Sociology as a method of approach and a body of knowledge differs from the other social sciences in that it emphasizes the "groupness" of human behavior. The basic argument advanced in this perspective is that human behavior is strongly contingent upon social norms and values that result from group interaction. This group-based (interpersonal) perspective is somewhat unlike the more individualistic (intrapersonal) emphasis associated with human behavior by some divisions of the social sciences. Economists, for example, tend to point out the utilitarian nature of human behavior, positing rational choice as the basis of such behavior (Rawls, 1992). They suggest that human beings calculate their choices and negotiate their responses to the various demands of their environment in terms of cost and benefit outcomes. In other words, an individual will most likely carry out and repeat a course of action he or she deems to be beneficial. On the other hand, if that individual does not consider the particular behavior to be beneficial, it will not be carried out, much less be repeated. However, while sociologists do not deny the role of rational choice as a feature of human activities, they do not hold it as the primary motivating force of these activities. Sociologists point to the fact that many human behaviors are carried out without regard to their value. Many people, for example, continue to adhere to social practices (e.g., cigarette smoking or hazing) that are clearly not in their best physical interest. Yet they are inclined to indulge in these practices, largely because of the weight of social expectations.

Emile Durkheim (1964), who in many ways can be seen as the premier architect of the sociological perspective, argues for an external locus for human activities. He maintains that social facts[2] which are group-produced and group-sustained phenomena constitute the mainspring of human conduct. In the development of his ideas on the forces that inform human behavior, Durkheim takes issue with the reigning theories of psychology and sociobiology of his time period. While psychology proposes that human behavior is due to psychological factors, such as the will and other characteristics of the mind, sociobiology suggests that biological principles, such as genetic predispositions and hormonal levels, are the real cause of human behavior. Contrary to both of these views, Durkheim argues that the ways in which people relate to the world around them (construct, sustain, or deconstruct that world) are socially rooted.

For example, Durkheim notes that the ways people fulfill their duties in their jobs and other personal relationships have all been given in the social expectations and established practices of their society. In other words, the

---

2. Durkheim (1964) defines social facts as "ways of acting, thinking, and feeling, external to the individual, and endowed with a power of coercion, by reason of which they control him" (p. 3).

ways people relate to their brothers, mothers, or bosses are largely deter-mined by the norms of the society in which they live. The key, therefore, to understanding human behavior lies in a study of social facts. In keeping with this Durkheimian logic, sociologists recognize that there is an objec-tive, socially-created reality in social facts that provides the impetus for and sustenance of human action and interaction.

This group-focused approach to human behavior seems to ignore the biblical view that each human is responsible for his or her actions (2 Cor. 5:10), however. While this is true to some extent, it is the contention of this author that the characterization of the sociological perspective as anti-biblical will not hold up upon closer inspection. In fact, in this study, I shall argue that the group focus of sociologists in their quest to understand human behavior and society is largely defensible within the biblical view of humans. This point will be articulated toward the end of this chapter as one of the principal reasons Christians ought to study sociology. But there are at least two other reasons for Christians to understand the human condition from the sociological perspective.

Rationale for the Study of Sociology

Sociology is a useful tool for Christians because (1) it provides an important account of the self and others, and (2) through it one can obtain a much-needed understanding of the social world. Of course, the position that sociology provides the only or even the best account of the human condition is not taken here. Human beings are far too complex to be reduced to a single disciplinary, perspectival explanation. Sociology is but one of several ways of viewing human beings.

The need for Christians to seek an authentic understanding of themselves and others derives in part from the commands of God to humans to "be fruitful and multiply..." (Gen. 1:28) and to love one another as they love themselves (Matt. 19:19). These injunctions loom even larger when viewed in the light of human beings bearing the image of God (Gen. 1:27). Indeed, to reproduce (multiply) selves created after the image of God and to love one's self and extend that love to others cannot be attempted on the basis of mere guesswork and uninformed emotions. Thorough and systematic efforts are required. Moreover, it would be enormously difficult for humans made in the image of God to reproduce themselves and truly love themselves and others without an authentic awareness of the self and others. Common-sense understanding would not suffice. Often such understandings display no more than a superficial, impressionistic grasp of the issues. In addition to inspired writings, we must draw upon the accumulated wisdom of the human race for clarity and direction.

Many people take their behavior for granted, seemingly unable to readily see their behavior within the multi-layered circumstances of their lives. Saddled with an individualistic ethos, most people seem to think of their behavior in terms of their personal qualities, thereby demonstrating a lack of the capacity to grasp the general in the particular, that is, to see themselves within the wider circumstances of their lives. In this they display a notorious innocence regarding the "thereness" component of their behavior. Yet this notion seems clearly biblical, in light of the Psalmist's suggestion that God will take note when He documents the lives of the people that "this man was born there" (Ps. 87:6). The implication here seems to be that God considers the place of a person's birth and his or her socialization experience to be important to his or her life activities and character formation. This position of the Psalmist is consistent with the sociological perspective, which pursues an understanding of the behavior of people within the context of their social locations.

The Sociological Imagination

C. Wright Mills, who drew upon and extended the Durkheimian notion of social facts, has given us perhaps the most insightful account of the "thereness" approach. Mills (1959) advances the notion of the "sociological imagination," which is critical to understanding that the behavior of humans is guided by the normative demands of their society. He suggests that one who possesses the sociological imagination is able to see how history and biography intersect in their impact upon the lives of people.

In Mills's (1959) own words, "the sociological imagination enables its possessor to understand the larger historical scene in terms of its meaning for the inner and the external careers of a variety of individuals" and "to grasp history and biography and the relations between the two in society" (pp. 65–66). Accordingly, Mills argues that any social investigation properly carried out will demonstrate a grasp of human conduct as a function of the intersection of history (those broad structural features within a society) and biography (the personal and more immediate circumstances of the lives of individuals).

It is these historical and biographical "thereness" factors that comprise the multi-layered circumstances of people's lives and against which sociologists seek to understand social behavior. It is also within this perspective that the forces underlying the varied patterns of behaviors that Christians manifest across cultural boundaries can be made. Consider the example of Adventist Christian men in the United States of America and in Northern Cameroon. While these two groups definitely share the same compelling worldview and are constrained by it in significant ways, they differ in some important ways. Adventist men in Northern Cameroon speak French, don Muslim-like robes to worship, and are likely to be married to wives chosen for them by their parents. On the other hand, Adventist men living in the United States of America speak English, wear a jacket and tie for worship services, and are most likely married to wives of their personal choice. Despite their common beliefs and values, these two groups differ in the ways they enact these beliefs and values, largely because of the social expectations of their respective societies.

The capacity to see people's behaviors in terms of the circumstances of their lives holds much significance for the practice of Christianity. Perkins (1987) has argued that the study of sociology leads to greater analytic clarity. He suggests that this clarity, coupled with the ability to communicate theoretical insights gained from the study of sociology, is invaluable to the realization and development of people's potential as beings made in the image of God. The insights and clarity of thought gained are especially valuable for a person's self-consciousness as well as his awareness of other humans. These provide the conditions that facilitate true love to self and others. Indeed, a person cannot genuinely love herself if she does not know herself; she is even less able to love others if she does not know them and the circumstances of their lives.

That the sociological perspective empowers people to meaningfully love others is ably brought out in the work of Michael Schwalbe (2001). This author suggests that sociological insights invest people with a "sociological mindfulness," which enables them to pay attention to the hardship and options of others. He notes that "if we observe how others' circumstances differ from our own we are more likely to show compassion for them and to grant them the respect they deserve as human beings, and less likely to condemn them unfairly" (p. 5). In other words, being sociologically mindful equips the Christian with the capacity of reflexivity (see Perkins, 1987). A reflexive Christian is one who is able to step outside one's social situation and frame of reference (his "thereness"), and "judge" oneself and others based on a careful and objective understanding of the facts. This ability to be reflexive is indispensable to a person's capacity to follow the golden rule, i.e., treating others as one wishes to be treated (Matt. 7:12). This is why Leming, DeVries, and Furnish (1989) argue that "the sociologically conscious Christian is better equipped to realize Shalom, to implement love and justice in the world" (p. 12).

Hence, whatever the term used to identify the insights gained from the study of sociology, there can be but little doubt, if any, that such a study increases the capacity to be more self aware and to be more other-sensitive and caring. To the extent that sociology facilitates the development of such capacity, its study is certainly justified for the Christian.

Another reason Christians should give sociology scholarly attention lies in the potential of the discipline to create an awareness of the varied ways in which the social world is conceived and constructed. This awareness is especially important to Christians for the empowerment it affords them to systematically engage scholarly discourse on the social world. Indeed, discourse on the origin, nature, and change of social patterns must not elude Christians. Christians are called upon "to appraise any new ethos that shapes the culture in which God calls believers to live" (Grenz, 1996, p. 167), "to demolish arguments and every pretension that sets itself up against the knowledge of God, and to take captive every thought to make it obedient to God" (2 Cor. 10:5).

This implies that Christians ought to be equipped in order to engage an offensive against ideas that stand opposed to God. This suggests, in Heddendorf's (1990) words, a "communication among persons who share their differing experiences of reality for the purpose of discovering some ultimate truth" (p. 191). In the process of the encounter, the tension between opposing views is addressed, giving rise to a new proposition, the synthesis. The principles that guide the process ensure that the best views presented in each of the positions advanced are retained and included in the new adopted position, while those that cannot stand the scrutiny of informed judgment are discounted.

Consistent with this spirit, Christians, in their effort to "demolish" arguments and take every thought captive, are expected to carefully evaluate the submissions of their non-Christian counterparts in order to retain whatever is salvageable therein. This demands that Christians exercise good judgment and display due civility when debating secular ideas. This will ensure that proponents of these ideas are not left to feel dejected or irate at the discounting of their ideas, without the sense of knowing that their works have been properly scrutinized and evaluated before they were thus treated. Fair play would have the secular researcher return like favor to the Christian researcher. Far from this approach being a compromise of principle, it represents not only scholarly courtesy but also the Christian way in which to deal with ideas that are antagonistic to truth.

For Christians to effectively engage the challenge of demolishing arguments and taking ideas captive, making them conducive to the glory of God, they first need to understand the relevant ideas and arguments. Specifically, they must understand the basis of the propositions advanced in the arguments to be demolished or preserved and be able to come up with informed, credible counter-propositions or justifications that result in the generation or adoption of a new, more defensible position. The objective of such an exercise, of course, is not to generate sterile theories that lead to endless strife, but rather, as the apostle Paul suggests in 2 Corinthians, to facilitate thoughtful obedience to God.

Further, this challenge of Paul to Christians to demolish arguments and take every thought captive suggests that Christians become the thought leaders of their society. This position harmonizes with Jesus' commission to his followers to be the light (Matt. 5:13) and the salt (Matt. 5:17) of the world. The assertion of Jesus in these verses may be construed as having relevance to all dimensions of the human condition, including the social, intellectual, physical, and spiritual. The implication therefore is that followers of Christ must be the means through which these dimensions in their operational forms in the society are flavored and preserved (the salt effect) and illuminated and explicated (the light effect). In these ways, Christians can demonstrate their faithfulness to their roles as the light and the salt of their society, respectively. True to these roles, Christians will become not only the stabilizing and preservative forces in their society but the meaning generators as well. As meaning generators, Christians will lead out in the creation of new knowledge providing answers to the many puzzling questions of their society in such areas as health, family life, and religious practice.

However, Christians will remain much challenged if they attempt to meet these functions without a thorough and authentic grasp of the theories and conceptual models that address the social patterns of their society. Yet Heddendorf (1990) has charged that "at a time when modern society staggers with the complexity of social life, Christian social thought remains largely naive and uncomprehending of these complexities" (p. 9). It is largely because of this deficit that Christians by and large have neglected (and in some cases abandoned) their light-bearing (meaning generating) roles and have contributed by their inaction to the proliferation of secular ideas antagonistic to biblical claims. Where sociology empowers Christians with an understanding of the social world, thereby facilitating the execution of their roles as thought leaders and light bearers of their society, its study is certainly justified.

Thus far, two reasons have been put forth for the necessity of Christians to engage in the study of sociology. The first reason pins the relevance of sociology to the Christian upon the knowledge of self and others it facilitates, thereby increasing the Christian's capacity for loving and serving others. In the second reason considered, it is suggested that sociology allows for an authentic and thorough grasp of the social world and that, as such, its study places the Christian in a position of empowerment to take every thought captive for the glory of God. Now a third and final reason is to be considered: the sociological unit of analysis, the group, is an eminently biblical theme; and because of this, the discipline stands deserving of the Christian's inquiry.

A Biblically-Based Unit Analysis

One of the critical decisions social scientists must make in their research endeavors relates to the unit of analysis. This term refers to the source from which the researcher intends to obtain the data for his or her study. Units of analysis include, but are not limited to, individuals, roles, personality types, institutions, regions, and groups. Kaplan (1968) considers units of analysis to be the "locus problem" of the research enterprise. He describes units of analysis as the "ultimate subject matter for inquiry" (p. 78). Once the unit of analysis is chosen, decisions regarding the research design and the method of analysis are made. While not denying the validity of other sources of data, sociologists have long considered the group the ultimate unit of analysis, and for good reason.

Once chosen, units of analysis are subject to two kinds of fallacies: ecological and individualistic. The individualistic fallacy occurs when the researcher uses data from one level of analysis and extrapolates the findings to another level. For example, suppose a researcher carried out a study to determine the attitude of young adults to abortion and found that young male adults in the Southern counties of the United States where the study was done were more pro-choice than pro-life. Now, the unit of analysis in this study is individual young adult. Findings should therefore be generalized to young adults. However, if the researcher concluded on the basis of her findings that Southern counties were more likely to adopt pro-choice policies than other counties, she would be committing the individualistic fallacy, drawing conclusions about county governments on the basis of individual data. The converse of this example is also possible, where a researcher could have committed the ecological fallacy by lifting data from county administrators, and then generalizing the findings to individual young adults. Both of these fallacies must be avoided, since they lead to a distortion of the facts.

The preferred sociological unit of analysis, the group, remains a firm basis upon which probable conclusions about individuals and other phenomena may be understandably reached. This argument draws on the logic of the systems theory (Goldenberg & Goldenberg, 2003), which posits that the whole is more than the sum of its parts, and that while the parts may be understood in terms of the whole, the opposite is not true. It is in this sense that Whitaker's assertion (cited in Olson and DeFrain, 2006, p. 64) becomes meaningful: "there are no individuals in the world—only fragments of families [groups]." The implication here is that the individual, while limited in his effect upon the group, cannot escape the impact of the group, in particular the family group; in fact, he is deeply influenced by his primary group background.

Therefore, the contention of those who argue that groups have no real existence apart from the individuals who comprise them ignores an important point, much as it seeks to isolate the identity of the individual outside the group context. Durkheim has made that point in insisting that the group is not limited to its constituent members, but becomes a new thing—a *sui generis*[3] reality, independent of its individual members (Durkheim, 1964). Thus, contrary to the views of those who would otherwise argue, groups are real and constitute a fundamental aspect of reality.

---

3. *Sui generis* reality: This Latin term conveys the idea that something is a reality in and of itself and cannot be reduced to its subunits without losing its essence.

The Biblical View of the Group

The position regarding the fundamental nature of the group is a pervasive biblical theme. This notion comes up early in the biblical account. When God had made the first human being, He declared him, along with the rest of His created works, to be "very good" (Gen. 1:31). Soon thereafter, He interjected that it was not good for the man to be alone (Gen. 2:17) and provided Adam a companion, Eve. But what could God mean by saying that the man was good, but yet that it was "not good" for him to be alone? The point of emphasis here is that the human person as a product of God's creation, given all his or her potential for creative expressions, is in an excellent state. However, human beings are not inanimate objects or will-less creatures; rather, they are beings endowed with the capacity for meaningful relationships. They will thus be hopelessly stifled and stagnated without the opportunity to fulfill their need for relationships. In this light, it is not good for human beings to live in isolation, without the benefit of interaction with others.

Many years ago, sociologist Charles Horton Cooley (1964) captured the essence of this thought when he noted that "a separate individual is an abstraction unknown to experience" (p. 36). What Cooley meant is that a developed and actualized individual is inconceivable outside of a group context. Humans do not fare well apart from the group. Indeed, some studies (Davis, 1940/2003; Rymer, 1994) have supported the idea that the actualization of our humanness is difficult to achieve outside of the group context. For example, both Davis's and Rymer's accounts of their two abused girl victims illustrate the impact of social isolation (aloneness) on human development. Davis's single subject was Anna. Born in 1932 to an unmarried, mentally-retarded mother, Anna was confined to an attic room because of her grandfather's rage over her illegitimate birth. Anna received little attention and just enough milk to stay alive. After five long years in this condition, with minimum contact from her mother and others, according to Davis, Anna was emaciated and unable to laugh, smile, show anger, or speak. Davis reported that after Anna was discovered and exposed to much social contact, she showed improvement in her social skills. She became more alert and was able to smile after about ten days of visits from him. She was able to walk after a year and to feed herself after a year and a half.

Somewhat similar to Anna's situation is Genie's. According to Macionis (1999), Genie was a thirteen-year-old girl from California. Her parents severely neglected and abused her in several ways, including locking her alone in the garage for extended periods. When discovered she was found to have the mental development of a one-year-old. In spite of intensive treatment by specialists, Genie improved only minimally, and her language skills remained that of a young child. These examples of the effect of social isolation on human subjects illustrate what happens to a person when he or she is deprived of the benefits of interaction with other humans.

One God in Three

The group reality must be appreciated not only for its relevance to human development but also for its apparent appropriateness in capturing the divine reality. In spite of its clear monotheistic ring, the biblical account seems uncompromised on the idea of God as a group. While God has been declared to be one God (Deut. 6:4; 1 Tim. 2:5), He has also been presented as a plurality of beings (Matt. 28:19; Eph. 4:5). These positions on the deity, while they seem to involve a contradiction of terms, become clearer within a wider sweep of Scripture.

Spouses become one flesh at marriage (Gen. 2:24; Matt. 19:5; Eph. 5:31), and Jesus prayed for His followers to be one (John 17:21). Paul (1 Cor. 12) presents the church with its plurality of members as one body, and Matthew (chapter 25) pictures the redeemed of the ages as a bride. Thus, the notion of oneness emerging from groupness seems clearly biblical. Yet, as evidenced by the experience of husbands and wives and of the followers of Christ, this group-based oneness does not translate to fusion of beings or personalities. Neither husbands and wives nor individual Christians are molded into a single entity at the point where oneness between them is reached.

What the notion of a triune (group) God seems to suggest is that the three members of the Godhead become joined in their relationship with each other on the basis of their common purpose, values, and interests. Furnish (1989) has suggested that a mystical oneness emerges when people interact in a group context. If this is true of human beings, how much more might it be illustrative of the oneness of the Godhead?

The point underscored by Scripture in the persistent image it portrays of "oneness" being a function of "groupness" is that reality is ultimately relational; it is within relationships, and in particular the group relationship, that reality is best conceptualized, accessed, and constructed. But this view does not sit well in cultures dominated by the Western individualistic notion of human nature. Bellah (1985) has suggested that this notion is best sum-marized by the Lockean concept of "ontological individualism" (p. 143), by which the individual is deemed to be prior to the group, and the group is seen to emerge upon the coming together of individuals, whose existence is independent of the group. "Invictus," a poem by Henley (1936), captures the spirit of this notion in its extreme implications of the self-determined individual who strives and triumphs alone. Henley writes:

> *It matters not how straight the gate,*
> *How charged with punishments the scroll,*
> *I am the master of my fate;*
> *I am the captain of my soul.*

Yet, an "individual-less" collective is not the ideal. The Christian world-view steers clear of this. What seems inescapable, however, is that God in whose image humanity has been created is communal, and humans are in essence social beings—made for God and for each other (Sire, 1990). That the group is the primary reality is the unyielding contention of the sociolo-gist—and of Scripture, too. It thus seems reasonable to conclude that, if only for its espoused unit of analysis—the group—sociology ought to find some place of importance in the Christian's scholarly inquiry. But sociology must be studied through the eyes of Christian understanding.

References

Bellah, R. H. (1985). *Habits of the heart: Individualism and commitment in American life*. Berkeley, CA: University of California.

Cooley, C. H. (1964). *Human nature and the social order*. New York: Schocken. (Original work published 1902)

Davis, K. (2003). Extreme isolation. In J. M. Henslin (Ed.), *Down to earth sociology: Introductory readings* (12th ed.). New York: Free Press, 133–142. (Original work published 1940)

Durkheim, E. (1964). *The rules of sociological method* (S. A. Solovay & J. H. Mueller., Trans.). E. G. Catlin (Ed.). Chicago: Chicago University Press.

Furnish, B. F. J. (1989). Are groups real? In M. R. Leming, R. G. DeVries, & B. F. J. Furnish (Eds.), *The sociological perspective: A value-com-mitted introduction*. Grand Rapids, MI: Academie Books.

Goldenberg, I., & Goldenberg, H. (2003). *Family therapy: An overview*. Pacific Grove, CA: Brooks/Cole.

Grenz, S. J. (1996). *A Primer on postmodernism.* Grand Rapids, MI: William B. Eerdmans Publishing Company.

Heddendorf, R. (1990). *Hidden threads: Social thought for Christians.* Dallas: Probe Books.

Henley, W. E. (1936). Invictus. In H. Felleman (Ed.), *The best loved poems of the American people.* New York: Garden City Books.

Kaplan, A. (1968). *The conduct of inquiry.* New York: Harper and Row.

Leming, M. R., DeVries, R. G., & Furnish, B. F. J. (Eds.). (1989). *The sociological perspective: A value committed introduction.* Grand Rapids, MI: Academie Books.

Macionis, J. J. (1999). *Sociology* (7th ed.). Upper Saddle River, NJ: Prentice Hall.

Maslow, A. H. (1970). *Motivation and personality* (2nd ed.). New York: Harper.

Mills, C. W. (1959). *The sociological imagination.* London: Oxford University Press.

Nohria, N., Lawrence, P., & Wilson, E. (2001). *Driven: How human nature shapes our choices.* San Francisco: Jossey-Bass.

Olson, D. H., & DeFrain, J. (2006). *Marriage and the family: Diversity and strengths* (5th ed.). Mountain View, CA: Mayfield Publishing Company.

Perkins, R. (1987). *Looking both ways.* Grand Rapids, MI: Baker Book House.

Pratt, D. (1994). *Curriculum planning: A handbook for professionals.* Fort Worth, TX: Harcourt Brace College Publishers.

Pring, R. (1987). *Personal and social education in the curriculum: Concepts and content.* London: Hodder and Stoughton.

Rawls, A. (1992). Can rational choice be a foundation for social theory? *Theory and Society, 21*(2), 219–241.

Ryan, R., & Deci, E. (2000). Self-determination theory and the facilitation of intrinsic motivation, social development, and well-being. *American Psychologist, 55*(1), 68–78.

Rymer, R. (1994). *Genie.* New York: Harper Perennial.

Schwalbe, M. (2001). *The sociologically examined life: Pieces of the conversation.* Mountain View, CA: Mayfield Publishing Company.

Sire, J. W. (1990). *Discipleship of the mind: Learning to love God in the ways we think.* Downers Grove, IL: InterVarsity Press.

Thompson, M., Grace, C., & Cohen, L. (2001). *Best friends, worst enemies: Understanding the social lives of children.* New York: Ballantine Books.

White, E. G. (1903). *Education.* Mountain View, CA: Pacific Press Publishing Association.

CHAPTER TWO

CHRISTIANITY AND THE SOCIOLOGICAL PERSPECTIVE: CONFLICT OR CONFLUENCE?

This chapter examines the sociological perspective in some detail. Circumstances that led to the development of the discipline are discussed. The particular theoretical perspectives that frame the discipline are developed against their larger philosophical underpinnings, such as social constructionism, positivism, and humanism. How the various theoretical perspectives both pose a threat to and provide support for the Adventist and broader Christian faith tradition is addressed.

Notwithstanding the benefits of studying sociology, the discipline presents fundamental challenges to the Christian worldview. Within the sociological argument are conceptual and philosophical eddies of which Christians must be aware, particularly those who wish to maintain a consistent and informed commitment to the church worldview. This chapter examines four such concepts: positivism,[1] humanism,[2] determinism,[3] and constructionism.[4] While these philosophical positions will be explored in terms of the challenge they pose to Christian thought, instances where they harmonize with the Christian perspective will be noted. How the Christian teacher can meet the challenge and transform the classroom into a faith-building experience will be addressed later in the book.

However, before examining these positions and pointing out where they harmonize with or diverge from the Christian perspective, the stage

---

1. Positivism: A method of inquiry based on sense impressions and the belief that human behavior can be predicted by the use of such a method of inquiry.

2. Humanism: The belief that human beings can realize their potentials independent of extra-human forces.

3. Determinism: The view that events and actions are caused by factors other than human free will.

4. Constructionism: The view that all realities, including moral reality, are constructed by humans.

must be set for this engagement by discussing the circumstances that gave rise to the emergence of sociology. In the process, this chapter will also examine the reputed anti-religion stance of sociology.

The Rise of Sociology

Developments of new theories or disciplinary perspectives are not disconnected, random occurrences. Rather, they emerge against the press of events and social currents that predate them. Within the logic of the scientific enterprise, things do not just happen—they are caused. Thus the rise of sociology as a discipline, with the particular perspective it brings to bear upon the study of society and human social relations, has been preceded by a set of identifiable, predisposing factors.

The events and ideas that lie behind sociology's evolution date back to early social critics and philosophers such as Aristotle and Plato. However, the more immediate circumstances that fueled the rise of the discipline are to be found in the aftermath of the French and Industrial Revolutions, the travels of Europeans to the New World, and the success of the natural sciences (Charon, 1999).

The French Revolution provided much cause for concern. Carried out under the motto of liberty, equality, and fraternity, the revolution drew on the ideas of the Enlightenment thinkers who sought to counteract the influence of traditional authority, particularly that of the church. Reasoning that societal order resulted from the rational mind of individuals rather than the collective will of institutions, disciples of the Enlightenment questioned the basis of the ranking ecclesiastical order that dominated society at the time. For these thinkers, ultimate power rested with the individual, not the collective. Therefore, the collectivist assumption that provided justification for the way society was organized was not to be tolerated. Because the individual was capable of making sense of social reality through the unaided powers of the mind, the Enlightenment thinkers reasoned that social institutions should be rejected if they did not correspond with rational principles. Preference was given to individual rationality.

This mindset created by the Enlightenment led not only to distrust of the established authority but also to military assaults on that authority. The resultant upheavals mounted to such highs that the Pope was taken captive by the French General, Berthier. This seriously disturbed the confidence and peace of mind of those who had placed their trust in the status quo.

Ritzer (1988) points out that the French Catholic revolutionary philosophers advanced the most extreme form of reaction to Enlightenment thought. These scholars lamented the erosion of social and political authority caused by the Enlightenment mindset. They were troubled by the undermining of the "sacred" values upon which, for them, the stability and preservation of the social order rested. The following ten points, adapted from Zeitlin (2001, pp. 63, 64), encapsulate their opposition to the ideas of the Enlightenment. They argued the following:

1. Society should be seen as an organic unity with its internal laws of development rooted in the past. It is a reality in and of itself and not merely another name for an aggregate of individuals.

2. Society is prior to individuals, and individuals are dependent upon society for the realization of their human potentials. Therefore, society does not derive its essence from individuals; rather, it is society that molds individuals through the instilling of moral values.

3. Individuals do not constitute the basic elements of society; without the guidance of society, which informs individual behavior through its institutions and the associated statuses and roles, individuals remain an abstraction. Thus individuals become useful in society only as they are positioned in specific statuses and roles.

4. Because the elemental parts of society—such as customs, beliefs, and institutions—are interdependent and interrelated, any reorganization of one element affects the effective functioning of the others.

5. Humans have fundamental needs realizable only through the various institutions of society. When these institutions malfunction and are rendered ineffective, the result is suffering and disorder.

6. All customs and institutions are functional; even those like prejudice, which appear to be harmful, can serve useful purposes.

7. Society thrives on the existence of small groups, the elementary forms of social life. Thus the family, neighborhood, religious groups, and other such groups provide the linchpin of human life.

8. Social organization is needed to preserve the older religious forms. Catholicism was to be preferred to Protestantism and the collective to the individual.

9. Contrary to the position of the Enlightenment thinkers, humans' needs for ritual, ceremony, and worship are necessary to the nonrational aspects of human society.
10. A hierarchical arrangement is needed as a basis for order and stability in the church, the family, and the state.

In summary, these propositions represent a strong statement against the extreme individualism promoted by Enlightenment thought and point the way back to the value of the collective in human society.

While the French Revolution elicited the aforementioned points, the process of European expansionism into the New World prompted new interest in explaining the dissimilarity between lifestyle patterns observed in the New World and those patterns the Europeans had left behind in their homelands. Coupled with this awakened curiosity were the disturbing consequences of the Industrial Revolution; though the Industrial Revolution brought many benefits to society, it also produced many troubling patterns.

The Industrial Revolution ushered in a type of alienation and competitiveness that is often found in modern capitalist economies, replacing the bondedness and harmony associated with the pre-modern social order. A rural lifestyle, in which people enjoyed commonly-held values, yielded to the search for a better life in the developing industrial towns of Europe. This rural-urban migration drift created a huge surplus in the labor force, resulting in levels of poverty hitherto unknown. The anonymity created by this vast meeting of strangers—rural folk from everywhere, seeking employment in the cities, many of whom must go without—resulted in an increase in social ills such as vagrancy and prostitution. While these conditions drove the scholars of the European nations, particularly in France, to look for answers to these worrying trends in their societies, the success of the natural sciences inspired them with hope of arriving at satisfactory answers.

Laying the Foundation: The Founding Fathers

Against this backdrop of despair and hope, Auguste Comte and the other founding fathers of sociology conceived and advanced their vision. Comte was among the first to advance the idea that society should be studied in the same way as the natural sciences. Accordingly, he embraced the mode of inquiry known as positivism, asserting that this held the key to righting the ills of society and ensuring its progress (see Ashley & Orenstein, 2005; Steinmetz, 2004). He was particularly displeased with the Enlightenment thinkers' overemphasis on pure rationality; he blamed this emphasis for the French Revolution and the chaos that revolution caused. However, while Comte's reaction to Enlightenment thinking identified him with some conservatives, the positivist solution he proposed deviated somewhat from the agenda of the die-hard conservatives. This was because his concern was aimed at rescuing "conservative ideas and concepts from their theologically reactionary context" (Zeitlin, 2001, p. 64). In light of this aim, Comte's positive philosophy was to become a major challenge to Christianity. This will be discussed more in the next section.

Of course, Comte was not the only scholar to be disturbed by the uncertainties spawned by the French and Industrial Revolutions. While Comte's reaction was to formulate a conceptual solution to the problems that resulted, Emile Durkheim (1915) was equally perturbed and reacted with a theoretical vision of his own. Durkheim differed little from Comte in his conception of social reality. He conceived of society not as a mere collection of individuals but as a reality in and of itself. For him, social order and human conduct were rooted in social facts and must be primarily accounted for in terms of forces outside the individual. He suggested that the social order resulted neither from the mental creation of individuals nor the imposition of super-human forces, but was a function only of human interaction. This particular view of Durkheim becomes, arguably, the basis of what we refer to today as social constructionism.

Karl Marx was another theorist whose insights were impacted by both counter-enlightenment and Enlightenment thoughts, as well as by the social ferment engendered by the revolutions. Whereas Comte castigated Enlightenment thinking for the furor of the French Revolution, Marx vented his rage towards the capitalist industrial system for reducing humans to "the level of animal laborans" (Marx, 1964, p. 30). He shared with the Enlightenment thinkers the view that humans were perfectible, being capable of attaining the highest level of creativity of thought and action. He thought, however, that the operation of the capitalist system and the alienation it engendered hindered this possibility.

Marx identified class conflict as a central characteristic of capitalism. Social inequality, he thought, was largely a measure of this conflict. He blamed the perpetuation of the capitalist system upon false consciousness forged and sustained by the influence of social institutions, including the church. However, Marx was convinced that the ripening contradictions of capitalism, coupled with the growing class awareness of the workers, would eventually usher in the demise of the capitalist system. This, he thought, would pave the way for the rise of a fairer, more egalitarian, socialist order. But neither Marx's class conflict theory nor his benign view of human nature proved to be a popular proposition. While his class analysis irked the power holders, his views of the self-determined perfectibility of human beings stood him at odds with the Christian worldview.

Max Weber is said to have carried on an ongoing debate with the ghost of Marx (Coser, 1971). He differed from Marx in the role he assigned ideas in the rise of capitalism in the Western World. He disputed Marx's negative view that religion was a reactionary force, and demonstrated that religious ideas were associated with the emergence of the materialistic capitalist system in the West (Weber, 1958). If Weber's position on religion's role in the development of Western capitalism earned him the favor of those who embraced religion as a way of life, his call for a value-free sociology did much to alienate that goodwill. Weber seemed convinced that "an empirical science cannot tell anyone what he should do—but rather what he can do" (Weber, 1949, p. 54). Weber's extreme empiricist stance rang true when he noted that "when a man of science introduces his personal value judgment, a full understanding of the facts ceases" (Weber, 1946, p. 152). Within this Weberian logic, the ideal sociologists are those who suspend their values in the practice of their discipline. While this may fit well with the logic of the positivist ideal of science, it certainly does not resonate well with Christians, who are called upon to live by their faith.

Much of classical and contemporary sociological thought reflects in one way or another the ideas of these four theorists. Comte produced the intellectual basis of empirical atheism with his positivist theory, Durkheim sowed the seeds of constructionism with his belief in a socially-constructed reality, Marx paved the way for a godless humanism, and Weber set the stage for a value-free sociology. The conceptual and philosophical trajectories of these theorists' ideas can be traced into the present.

Sociological Challenges to Christianity

The opening paragraph of this chapter identified positivism, humanism, determinism, and constructionism as major challenges sociology poses to the Christian perspective. Yet these philosophical positions are seldom, if ever, explicit in current introductory sociology texts. Most of these texts tend to frame the discipline in terms of three broad paradigms: structural functionalism, symbolic interactionism, and the conflict perspective (to be discussed later). Insofar as these paradigms serve to identify various angles from which to view the discipline, their usefulness is to be applauded. What often escapes the attention of beginners to the field of sociology, however, are the assumptions these overarching perspectives convey about human nature and the world. Yet it is on the basis of such assumptions that we must trace the degree to which the sociological perspective and the Christian worldview are compatible. Hence, in the next section I will analyze the degree of divergence/convergence that exists between sociology and the Christian worldview. An examination of the overarching assumptions that subsume these two metaviews regarding the image of humans and the nature of the world will facilitate this analysis.

Metaviews (broad overarching positions held about a subject) on humans and the world in which they live are responses to the philosophical questions of epistemology and metaphysics. Epistemology is concerned with the claim of how we know something, whereas metaphysics inquires into what exists. Scholars who seek to understand what exists are in fact attempting to account for the nature of reality. In this regard, they not only suggest what exists but how it exists and what valid statements can be made about it (Perkins, 1987).

Some Basic Assumptions of Christianity

All lasting systems developed around the fulfillment of basic human needs (economic, educational, or religious) are based on explicit and implicit assumptions regarding the source of knowledge (epistemology) and the nature of being (metaphysics). These assumptions, often spoken of as worldviews, form the life core of these systems and give them their mark of identity. Thus Christianity, notwithstanding its varied forms of expression, is undergirded by basic assumptions about humans and the world. To this end, Migliazzo (1993) has suggested that the following seven assumptions underlie the Christian world view:

1. God has created all things and created them good.
2. God's Creation is purpose driven.
3. Because of their rational, emotional, physical, and spiritual capacities, humans are a special part of God's creation, distinctly different from other created beings.

4. God is holy and loving and cares deeply for His Creation.
5. God's holiness and love mean that He is both just and compassionate toward His Creation.
6. Despite the sinfulness of humans, which has corrupted God's Creation, there is still intrinsic worth in the created works of God.
7. God intervened in human history through His Son Jesus Christ, whose death and resurrection healed the rift between sinful humans and God, thereby satisfying God's demand for justice and giving proof of His love. God's spoken and written words to humans contain what they need to know to be restored to a right relationship with God, other humans, and to the rest of God's creation.

Basic Assumptions of Sociology

As previously discussed, the sociological perspective, variously labeled as the "sociological imagination" (Mills, 1959) and "sociological mindfulness" (Schwalbe, 2001), places human conduct principally within the external and constraining forces of the social facts of thinking, feeling, and acting. From this Durkheimian standpoint, human behavior is itself a social fact, explainable only in terms of other social facts. Thus, some have characterized the perspective as socially deterministic, meaning that it allows little room for the expression of humans' free will. But sociologists have been able to forge varied theoretical insights against the broad vision of the discipline, depicting two contrasting images of humans. These images are portrayed in the three overarching paradigms of structural functionalism, symbolic interactionism, and the conflict perspective (sometimes referred to as conflict functionalism). These paradigms make assumptions about humans and their society that largely remain veiled in introductory sociology texts. However, the burden here lies in underscoring the epistemological and metaphysical implications of these paradigms. Therefore, for discussion purposes, the central philosophical underpinnings with which they are associated (positivism and humanism) have been isolated. In Table 2.1, these terms are matched against the three generally accepted paradigms, indicating where they constitute the assumptive base of the said paradigms.

Table 2.1
Types of Sociology and Related Paradigms

Types of Sociology	Sociological Paradigms
Positivistic	Structural functionalism Conflict perspective
Humanistic	Symbolic interactionism

Positivistic (Naturalistic) Sociology and Assumptions

Auguste Comte's ambition for the new discipline he created was that it should be patterned after the natural sciences, physics in particular. Thus, sociology was to facilitate the discovery of the objective social laws that underlie the variation of social phenomena. Disturbed as he was by the metaphysics of the Enlightenment thinkers and the French Revolution, which he believed was caused by the Enlightenment, Comte (1855) sought resolution in the positivism of his own making.

Comte described in his law of three states[5] what was for him the path of human hope and progress; he also addressed the questions of being and how humans come to know things. Human beings, Comte thought, had progressed through the theological stage, were confronting the metaphysical stage during his time, and were headed for the final stage of positive science, when, he felt, sociologist priests would rule society.

Had it not been for its inherent presuppositions regarding humans and nature, this eschatological vision of Comte might have had little for Christians to complain about. But Comte's positivistic sociology is grounded in several presuppositions, some of which are inconsistent with the fundamental claims of the Christian worldview. An examination of the core assumptions of positivism will reveal this.

Paul Tibbetts (1982) observes that the debate over positivism has been unabated ever since Comte's publication of *Positive Philosophy* in the 1840s. Tibbetts has compiled several assumptive claims of positivism.

---

5. In what he calls the law of three states, Comte describes the stages through which human knowledge has evolved, based on how social and natural phenomena are accounted for. These include the theological (accounts for events in terms of the supernatural), the metaphysical (accounts for reality with the aid of pure rationality), and the positive (scientific account of reality).

In condensed and simplified form, his positivist view of sociology would suggest the following ideas:

1. The only defensible explanation of an event in science consists of examining that event against the impact of empirical, independent variables. In other words, scientific explanations must be based on factors that can be grasped by the senses.

2. Metaphysical claims (those lying beyond the reach of empirical observations) cannot be the basis of valid statement about the world. Put another way, any claim that cannot be supported by sense impressions must be discounted.

3. All observations in science must be stated in language that flows from properties of the physical world.

4. In order for a proposition to be empirically meaningful it must be capable of verification and the way in which it can be verified must be clearly stated. Of course, the basis of verification must be on the basis of phenomena that can be accessed by the senses.

5. Conceptual definitions must be matched by a set of operations measurable in terms of sensory observations.

6. Phenomenalism is a necessary condition for verification, that is, the belief that only that which is manifested in experience is worth recording as data. Opinions concerning super-empirical entities should be deemed untrustworthy. Beliefs in God and a spiritual reality are therefore thrown out.

7. A division must be maintained between questions of facts and questions of values. This position is captured in Popper's (1963) suggestion that the "task of scientific discussion is to fight against the confusion of value-spheres…to separate scientific evaluations from questions of truth" (p. 97).

8. Distinct lines must be drawn between the rules that govern the discovery of scientific patterns and that inform their verification. The latter must ultimately be established through a community of scientific inquirers.

While these assumptions buttress the scientific paradigm, they leave little room for a super empirical reality. As such they are not supportive of a religious worldview: in fact, they are antagonistic to it. Certainly, Christians will find troubling the call to exclude all claims that cannot be empirically verified. They are equally likely to view with suspicion the suggestions that "opinions concerning super-empirical entities should be deemed untrustworthy" (op. cit. #6). Social theorizing is limited to the sensory realm by the position that the only legitimate explanation of an event is to be found through analysis of the empirical variables affecting that event. It thus discounts a non-sensory supernatural reality and to that extent the Christian's belief in the reality of a transcendent God. Additionally, it undermines the Christian's worldview claim of a super-empirical divine Other who intervenes in human affairs.

While Tibbetts (1982) claims that all of the assumptions of positivism have been under attack in one way or other, Poloma (1980) points out that Comte's naturalistic (positivistic) sociology has been dominant in both the areas of structural sociology and behavioristic psychology. Structural sociology appears in current sociological texts under the labels of structural functionalism and the conflict perspective, where a sharp distinction is made between the two in terms of the view each portrays of societal order and change.

Whereas structural functionalists represent societal order as resulting from the willing compliance of social actors, conflict theorists describe that order as a function of the coercion of powerful others in the society. Structural functionalists thus see change as adaptive and not transformational and revolutionary, as is the position embraced by the conflict theorists. However, as earlier indicated, what seldom receives any coverage in the discussion of these paradigms in introductory sociology texts is the assumption these paradigms make about the nature of human beings.

Positivistic Sociology Confronts Christian Worldview

Both the structural functionalist and the conflict paradigms display a rather passive, mechanistic view of humans. These paradigms suggest that social order results from the predictable reaction of social actors to the empirical conditions of their environment. People are either instilled with the values and norms of their society from which constraints they act (the structural functionalist view), or they are coerced by the powers that be to behave in ways that conform to a predetermined social order (the conflict theorist view). In these ways the stability and predictability of the social order are supposedly ensured.

In light of the above views, humans are either trained or forced to be compliant. While these positions are consistent with conventional wisdom, they are ultimately discordant with the biblical view of human behavior. The implication is that humans are at best manipulable creatures, incapable of originating actions outside of environmental constraints. This conveys an image of humans as creatures whose behaviors are determined—caused—by factors other than their free choice.

One would be hard put to deny evidences of the impact of external constraints on human behavior, whether those constraints are internalized as norms and values or more directly exercised as force. But it is the degree of determinism implied by positivist sociology that sets the discipline at odds with the Christian worldview. Determined behavior removes from the actor any responsibility for his or her behavior. As such, blame for misconduct must be placed elsewhere. Extending the logic of this argument to the phenomenon of sin demands that culpability for sin be attributed to someone or something other than the sinner. This, of course, denies the free will of humans and suggests that God is to be blamed for the act of sin. Thus, both the conflict and structural functionalist perspectives fail to account for the creative capacity of the individual. Human beings thus stand passive and robot-like, with their God-endowed, free will capacity much compromised.

Positivistic Sociology Facilitates the Christian Worldview

However, we may yet glean insights into the Christian worldview from the positivist argument of Comte and the derived accounts of social order from the conflict and structural functionalist perspectives. Positivism, insofar as it points to an objective reality, although empirical in nature, lends itself as a defense platform for the Christian claim of a God whose existence and will remain independent of human construction. Such a perspective makes allowance for the recognition of moral values as more than a social construction. Additionally, the positivist's deterministic interpretation of human conduct must necessarily imply that social conduct derives its energy from an extra-individual source. For the structural functionalist, that energy-providing source is the various social institutions through which humans are equipped with the constraining values of society. From the conflict paradigm standpoint, that source is some powerful "other" in the society.

Christians have similarly identified an external source of their strength and empowerment. In fact, Jesus reminds us that without Him we can do nothing (John 15:5). And the Apostle Paul, capturing this reality in personal terms, notes that he has been crucified with Christ but nevertheless lives on, because Christ lives in him (Gal. 2:20). This, however, should not be understood as a unilateral invasion and control of the Christian's life by Christ. Paul dismisses any such view in his suggestion that we become servants only to whom we will our lives in obedience (Rom. 6:16). In fact, the biblical view of humans gives much more agency to humans than to present them as beings under the unilateral control of others, even God. Nevertheless, positivistic sociology, in locating the driving force of behavior outside the individual, approaches congruence with the Christian perspective, which recognizes God's power as the source of the Christian's empowerment (Phil. 4:13). Both viewpoints emphasize the external nature of humans' empowerment.

Humanistic Sociology

As previously mentioned, the early beginnings of the humanistic trend in sociology can be traced to the works of Marx, and to a lesser extent Durkheim. Marx, with his espousal of the Enlightenment notion of the perfectibility of the individual, saw human beings as inherently good and capable of the highest attainment possible. However, he thought that humans were restrained from such realization because of their exploitation by the ruling class. Durkheim, though he argued for the externality of the driving force of human behavior, was not truly a positivist. In his *Elementary Forms of Religion* (1915), he has demonstrated that social reality and valid knowledge are the outcome of human interaction rather than the mere perception of the individual mind (Rawls, 2004).

Besides the foregoing early contributors to the humanistic sociological theme, a number of others (Berger, 1963; Bierstedt, 1974; Mead, 1934) have contributed to this school of thought. Unlike the passive, reactive image of humans implicit in the positivist sociological model, the humanistic model conveys a less deterministic, more creative view of humans. The strong emphasis on objectivity and value neutrality evident in the positivist version is replaced by an embrace of the relevance of the subjective and a focus on the totality of the human experience.

Assumptions of Humanistic Sociology

Tibbetts (1982) has summarized the salient underlying features of the humanistic sociological type. In simplified form, the humanist type has these features:

1. Human beings are self-determined with the capacity to act as autonomous agents, capable of acting rationally and purposely toward freely-chosen goals. (The suggestion here is that human behavior is not determined.)

2. Sociology can facilitate the emancipation of humans from coercive and alienating economic and ideological forces.

3. Human emancipation from alienating forces of society can be realized through increased self-awareness of their motives, values, and the various forces that facilitate and limit human expression.

4. The liberation achieved through self-awareness can lead to a new appreciation for the relationship between society and human action.

5. "Scientism" is denied, in particular the idea that science alone has the genuine methods and techniques for understanding society.

6. All science, be it social or physical, is value driven, and does not fit the objective value-neutral image positivists attribute to it.

7. In light of number six, social research cannot be carried out in a value-free context.

8. The intentional, subjective, interpretive aspects of human life cannot be ignored or seen as simply having no real social basis.

Humanistic sociology, with its free will, value-relevance, and anti-scientism stance, serves to align the discipline with the Christian worldview on humans. But its attribution of self-creative and redemptive powers (see numbers one, two, and three above) to the awakened consciousness of humans positions it against the Christian worldview. According to this perspective, human beings seem supreme; from them originate all the ideas, strategies, and schemes needed to order the world and facilitate their own actualization. (Numbers one and three above imply this.) The source of freedom and progress is within humans, not external to them. Humanists thus underscore the human-originated nature of ideas and social patterns. Societal patterns, including human values, are nothing more than expressions of human creative genius, and humans have become their own savior. Marx suggests this idea when he observes that for humans "to enter the domain of freedom is to begin consciously to determine their fortune" (Zeitlin, 2001, p. 148).

Thus for Marx, anything that takes away from this self-determining human activity obstructs their natural unfolding. In this light, Marx sees

religion as a human creation; he also sees it as a state of false consciousness, in that it "is the illusory sun about which man revolves so long as
he does not revolve about himself" (Ashley & Orenstein, 2005, p. 199).
Marx argues that religion is no more than an instrument of oppression in
the hand of the powerful. In his configuration, religion is a form of human
alienation in that humans' own creation now confronts them as an alien
power. It is not, as Christians would see it, the expression of the human/
divine encounter, i.e., God fulfilling Himself in humans and establishing
His kingdom on earth.

Humanism in Symbolic Interactionism

Humanistic sociology's implicit denial of the supernatural as a source
of value indicates the extent to which it stands brazenly opposed to the
Christian worldview. Yet newcomers to the field of sociology embrace
this major sociological strand under the theoretical paradigm of symbolic
interactionism with but little awareness of its philosophical implications.

The symbolic interactionist paradigm focuses upon the interactive, process-oriented, and emergent nature of societal order. Blumer (1969), one of
the chief architects of this paradigm, portrays it in terms of its three main
assumptions: (1) humans act toward things on the basis of the meanings
that the things have for them, (2) meanings are derived from social interaction, and (3) meanings are handled in and modified through an interpretive
process in dealing with the things that are encountered.

It is not the interactionist's focus on human creative capacity per se
that places it at odds with the Christian worldview; it is rather its social
construction emphasis. In their attempt to avoid the passive, creature-like
image of humans portrayed by positivist sociology, interactionists have
blundered into the opposite extreme by presenting humans as sovereign,
God-like creators. Nowhere is this more evident than in the concept of the
social construction of reality.

The Social Construction of Reality

Proponents of the social construction of reality theory (such as Rawls,
and Berger and Luckman) argue that all meaning-based reality originates
with human interaction. According to this view, ideas and systems of knowledge are deemed to have emerged from the concrete, observable, social
practice of everyday life (Rawls, 1996), rather than from an extra-empirical

realm, that is, from a supernatural source. In the light of this position, beliefs in biblical revelation as a source of knowledge must be discounted.

Berger and Luckman (1966) provide perhaps the best account of how the process of the social construction of reality works. They identify three stages in the process that characterize the interaction between humans and their society. The reciprocity is such that both human social life and society itself are produced and reproduced in the process.

The first phase of the process is described as externalization, referring to those activities through which humans construct their social world. These activities include the generation of ideas, the creation of policies, and the development of the norms and values. The second phase, objectivation, refers to the means by which the very ideas, policies, norms, and values that people have created come to be regarded as having a life of their own. In other words, these externalized products are treated as if they have always existed apart from their human creators. Berger and Luckman (1966) refer to the final stage as internalization. During this phase, these externalized and objectified products become the code of conduct to be studied, taught, and cherished as ideals. This process of the social construction of reality is ongoing and determines the production and reproduction of the social order.

This point can be illustrated with a current example. The laws that the U.S. Congress may now be in the process of making are an example of the externalization phase. Once these laws are enacted and placed on record, they become objectified, that is, they are treated as being independent of the lawmakers, and are respected and obeyed by all, including the lawmakers themselves. Finally, when the said laws are used as the basis for settling disputes, and are taught to the citizens, they have reached the phase of internalization.

The social construction of reality per se does not present a problem to the Christian worldview, though some may so argue. It is rather the epistemological and metaphysical connotations associated with that term that should be the source of concern to Christians. The social construction of reality is almost always taken to mean that reality is relative and that it is colored by and is limited to the particular characteristics of the social situation in which it was constructed. It is in this connection that the Christian teacher can show that there is an objective "truth" that comes from a knowledge of God, even though humans never fully apprehend it.

The Social Construction of Knowledge

One of the critical questions social constructionists address regards the source of knowledge. This question has received various treatments in the sociology of knowledge literature. Karl Marx (1964), for example, saw knowledge as rooted in the material conditions of life. He argued that it is social being (the material conditions of life) that determines social consciousness (ideas, beliefs, etc.). He maintained that all knowledge, except scientific knowledge and that of the emancipated proletariat, reflects the interest of the dominant class in society. Such class-derived knowledge is nothing more than ideology, ideas that explain and justify the current class arrangement. Thus, Marx would argue that the only authentic knowledge emerges from the scientific process and the experience of the liberated proletariat.

Max Scheler (1980) explained social construction somewhat differently. For him, there is an absolute order of ideal factors (the superstructure) that exists in the form of values, ideas, and eternal essences. He reasoned that ideal factors are accessible through real factors (the substructure) such as drives for food, sex, and power and that these factors give rise to a particular perspective. Real factors occur in each age and culture to facilitate access into the absolute realm. But Scheler maintained that the perspective gained with the end of these natural factors is only partially true.

Karl Mannheim (1936) aimed to overcome both absolutism and relativism. Mannheim asserted that absolutism was subscribed to by those who were "unable to look life in the face" (p. 87) for fear of losing their sense of certainty. He rejected relativism for its skeptical and nihilistic streaks, advancing instead the notion of relationalism, in which truth is acknowledged in terms of the context in which it becomes known. The subtle nuances in the articulation of these three views of knowledge notwithstanding, it is not difficult to detect the common thread of cultural relativity running through each.

Cultural Relativity and Metaphysical Relativism

Some Christians have taken the position that cultural relativity, a pervasive theme of postmodernism, implies that no universal standards guide issues of right or wrong. This, they say, undermines the Christian worldview. Cultural relativists work out ideas within their various cultural settings, with the result that the very idea of an absolute God, objective of humans'

construction, is compromised. Moberg (1962) captures this line of thinking, noting that "since each group has its own conception of deity, there are
many gods, none of which is universal and all of which are true" (p. 35).
In other words, cultural relativity does away with the idea of an absolute
God, much as it explains away universal standards of morality.

The fundamental premise of the cultural relativist's argument regarding God and transcendent truths is flawed, however. The suggestion
inherent in the logic is that God amounts to no more than our perception
of Him; so to the extent that various collectives of people perceive Him
differently, He becomes only what He is thought to be—no more, no less.
This logic, if followed through to its end, falls apart. For example, the
many opinions and views expressed about President Bill Clinton while
he was in office did not change him into many Bill Clintons. Indeed,
various perceptions of him proliferated during his trial, but these did not
change him ontologically; his objective self and being remained—only
perceptions of him varied.

Variation of perceptions about God by cultures and situations does not
change God ontologically. It does not alter who He is objectively, only
what and who He is perceived to be culturally and situationally. Therefore,
the varied versions rendered about who and what God is should not be the
source of the Christian's worry. Indeed, one might expect that the cultural
facilities by which people are aided in their interaction with God will, to a
large extent, determine their perception of Him. But this is quite different
from saying that God is only what He is thought to be, a position embraced
by the metaphysical relativist.

Metaphysical relativism holds that the essence of truth itself is relative.
Those who embrace this position do not subscribe to a transcendent truth
reality since, for them, all truth originates with human construction. And
because social constructionism is context-based, truth reality itself and not
just the perception of truth reality necessarily varies by context. This position
stands opposed to the Christian worldview claim of absolute, transcendent
truth, and as such is kept at bay by Christian sociologists. These sociologists subscribe to the timeless and eternal relevance of truth, personified in
Jesus and enshrined in Scripture. Absolute truth for Christian sociologists,
therefore, exists in its own right, transcendent and independent of human
construction and perception. It is this insight that Christian sociology teachers can offer their students.

However, whether humans attempt to understand absolute reality or seek to construct their own reality, their efforts are necessarily relative. Finite humans in their quest to conceptualize absolute truth (God and His created works) will ever come up short because of their own finitude. They cannot produce anything that is not conditioned by the cultural limitations of their society. In this light, Christian sociologists are not reluctant to acknowledge the relative nature of both perceived truth and socially constructed reality, even as they maintain belief in a transcendent God reality.

This position regarding the relative nature of perceived truth at the human level is consistent with the writings of Ellen White (1888). Throughout her prophetic insights, she suggests that absolute, objective truth is beyond the full knowledge of humans. For example, she points out that the unfolding years of eternity "will bring richer and still more glorious revelations of God and Christ." "As knowledge is progressive," she notes, "so will love, reverence, and happiness increase" (p. 410). This position harmonizes with that of the Apostle Paul, who describes human knowledge as partial and suggests that we will ever see "as through a glass darkly" the things we encounter, until we see Jesus face to face (1 Cor. 13:12).

Christian sociologists are, therefore, not naive to the fact that humans' view of absolute truth and their construction of reality are shaped by their own finitude and the limitations of the social contexts in which they transact. Because they accept that situational constraints influence humans' perception of truth, they are able to make sense of the multiple views of God and other truth realities evident among the various groups within the religious community. Groups even of the same denominational affiliation, depending on their particular socio-historical contexts, tend to forge different mental images of God and to develop liturgical forms consistent with these images. For example, given their socio-historical experience, African Americans seem more likely than other ethnic groups in the United States to conceive of God as a liberator. In fact, many of the Negro spirituals mirror such an image. This is perhaps the reason that some African-American congregations tend to take on a more celebrative character than those of others.

Further evidence of the impact of culture and social location on our sense of propriety can be seen in the ways people in different social contexts dress and entertain themselves. Depending on their social locations, some Christians view going to the movies as out of place while others, of the same denominational affiliation but from a different social context, are amused at such concerns. Some view the use of jewelry as improper, while others do not, yet this is not to be taken to mean that context justifies the Christian's participation in any and every social practice. The Christian's acceptance of and participation in the cultural norms and values of her society should always be informed by scriptural principles.

Despite their awareness of the demands that culture and place make upon human conduct, Christian sociologists, particularly Adventist sociologists, remain deeply cognizant of divine absolutes enshrined in the Decalogue and other biblical principles by which Christians must order their lives. They believe that these absolutes constitute the very bedrock of the moral code. Thus, while Christian sociologists are sensitive to the operational norms, placing value on them, they still uphold the moral code of Scripture as the ultimate standard by which these norms should be evaluated.

Some of the challenges a humanistic version of sociology poses for Christians have just been examined. These challenges included the idea of a socially-constructed reality and the social construction process. Cultural relativity and metaphysical relativism were discussed, with special note being taken that it is metaphysical relativism that poses the real problem for Christians.

Contribution of Humanistic Sociology
to the Christian Worldview

Poloma (1980) suggests that neither the positivist nor the humanist strain of sociological thought lends support to the Christian worldview. While this suggestion has merit, these thought models may yet be made to serve Christianity. It is true that if we delimit positivist sociology to its empiricist claim and its "creature" image of humans on one hand and humanistic sociology to its emphasis upon the perfectibility notion and its "creator" image of humans on the other, then these variants of the sociological perspective will hardly pass Christians' muster. However, as has been argued earlier in respect of positivistic sociology, we can yet glean insights into the Christian worldview on the basis of these thought models. There are at least two examples that illustrate this in the instance of humanistic sociology.

First, humanistic sociology stands amenable to the biblical perspective insofar as it seeks to point out that humans are more than mere "stimulus response" determinable creatures but rather are beings with the capacity to innovate and create meanings. That human beings were meant to be meaning generators is indicated by God's call to Adam to participate in the naming of His creation (Gen. 2:19). Indeed, to participate in naming something is to engage in an activity that is both creative and innovative. Such an activity consists of generating categories that are appropriate fits for the material as well as the non-material aspects of the world. In this process, not only the flora and fauna but also the related abstract properties and processes are paired with names and meanings. In a real sense it is the work that botanists, biologists, psychologists, and sociologists do in their knowledge-generation activities.

The naming of the world is of special importance, and it takes place at various levels of the church and the wider society as one of the means by which order is created and sense is made of the world. Researchers accomplish this task whenever they come up with new findings. Committees carry it out when they generate new ideas and structure these into new policies and procedures, aimed at facilitating the smooth operations of the church and the wider society. Can we imagine social development and progress without the naming and meaning-generation process?

Second, the symbolic interactionist's emphasis on the process-oriented nature of reality sheds light on the Seventh-day Adventist Christian's belief regarding salvation. Seventh-day Adventist Christians see salvation in terms of a three-phase process that begins with justification when the unmerited righteousness of Christ is imputed to the sinner and the sinner receives full salvation. Seventh-day Adventists believe, however, that the sinner who opts out of the relationship with Christ can forfeit this unmerited gift. Salvation results not so much from a thing applied but rather from an interactive relationship. What this suggests is that the application of Christ's blood in the salvific process transcends its literal meaning and is rather symbolic of the empowerment Christ makes available to us in our interactive relationship with Him. Sanctification, the second phase of the process, describes this relationship as a lifelong process. This position avoids the "once saved always saved" notion, which implies a unilateral act of God in saving the sinner, even against the sinner's will. Thus, the symbolic interactionist sociological frame of reference lends to the view Seventh-day Adventists embrace on salvation. (See Chapter 5 for a more expanded discussion.)

Explained Variance: The Inadequacy of the Scientific Method

Few, if any, Christians will doubt that sin has infected every aspect of human activities, including social theorizing. Consequently, no foolproof theoretical model exists that flawlessly captures reality, much less absolute, objective reality. The task of social theorizing is made very demanding by the fact that humans must overcome their particular conditionings and transcend their biased lenses in an effort to objectively integrate and report observed patterns not readily conformable to their culturally derived perspectives. The degree to which this is possible is still a matter of speculation.

But researchers of the positivistic sociological orientation seem confident that with their grounding of all reality in the empirical, and in their use of the associated naturalistic method of investigation, they are well on their way to plumbing the depths of objective reality. From a positivist sociological standpoint, reality resides only within the frame of the empirical; by implication, humans have all that is required to isolate, explain, manipulate, and predict observed phenomena. The ontological leap required to reach this positional certitude is often little appreciated, however. Positivists make the untested assumption (of course by faith) that empirical reality is all there is; then they proceed to castigate those who have committed to a belief in a transcendent non-empirical reality for not proving their case. Christians admittedly cannot prove, given the canons of scientific inquiry, that God exists; neither can the positivist prove that He does not exist and that reality does not transcend the empirical plane. Further, the very standard by which the positivists attempt to demonstrate their success at capturing empirical reality seems inadequate.

Empirical Evidence and Variance Explained

Social researchers who follow the quantitative/empirical tradition use model specification to ensure that social phenomena are adequately accounted for. In this exercise, a dependent variable, say crime commission, is seen as a function of a set of empirically-measurable independent variables. For example, education, religious orientation, and the ability to problem solve may be specified as predictors of crime commission. A properly specified model will include all theoretically-relevant independent variables, while omitting those that are theoretically implausible.

The value of a well-specified conceptual model lies in the amount of explained variance it captures. Explained variance gives us an idea as to how much of the variation of the dependent variable is accounted for by the specified independent variables. The greater the variance explained, the greater the explanatory power of the model. Thus, a model that accounts for 100 percent of the variance of the dependent variable is considered the best-specified model.

However, the findings of past and current empirical research remain far from this ideal. A random check of eleven empirical studies reported in the *American Journal of Sociology* (AJS) from 1992 to 2000 reveals an average variance explained of 16.5 percent, with a spread of 5 percent to 47 percent (see Table 2.2). If this is an indicator of how well researchers are able to explain social reality from a naturalistic standpoint, then much work remains to be done. Even with thriftiness in model specification, the vast percentages of variances left unexplained by the adopted models of these studies seem to constitute a forceful appeal to the empiricist to come up with better-fitting models. However, given the care and academic rigor generally exercised in arriving at analytic models, this may yet be a wake-up call to social scientists steeped in the empiricist logic to consider the possibility of a non-empirical source of impact. The metaphysical claim that empirical reality is all there is seems weakly supported by research models informed by such a claim. This book suggests ways a Christian sociologist can look beyond mere empirical reality.

Table 2.2
Selected *AJS* Articles and Patterns of Variance Explained

Article	Year	Variance Explained
Reflected Appraisals, Parental Labeling, and Delinquency: Specifying a Symbolic Interactionist Theory *by Ross L. Matsueda*	1992	.13
Successful Aging: A Life-Course Perspective on Women's Multiple Roles and Health *by Phyllis Moen, Donna Dempster-McClain, and Robin M. Williams, Jr.*	1992	.10
Gender, Parenthood, and Job-Family Compatibility *by Jennifer Glass and Valerie Camarigg*	1992	.06

Article	Year	Variance Explained
Young White Adults: Did Racial Attitudes Change in the 1980s? *by Charlotte Steeh and Howard Schuman*	1992	.05
Embedded Altruism: Blood Collection Regimes and the European Union's Donor Population *by Kieran Healy*	2000	.08
The Evolution of Sex Segregation Regimes *by Mariko Lin Chang*	2000	.07
Risk and Trust in Social Exchange: An Experimental Test of a Classical Proposition *by Linda D. Molm, Nobuyuki Takahashi, and Gretchen Peterson*	2000	.08
Institutions, Technical Change, and Diverging Life Chances: Earnings Mobility in the United States and Germany *by Thomas A. DiPrete and Patricia A. McManus*	1996	.32
Culture, Class, and Connections *by Bonnie H. Erickson*	1996	.217
Engineering Growth: Business Group Structure and Firm Performance in China's Transition Economy *by Lisa A. Keister*	1998	.24
Defended Neighborhoods, Integration, and Racially Motivated Crime *by Donald P. Green, Dara Z. Strolovitch, and Janelle S. Wong*	1998	.47

Although Christian sociologists utilize the positivist claim of an independent objective reality to formulate discussion on the Christian's proposition of a transcendent God, they are ever mindful of the limitations of this model in light of its efforts to bracket out the non-empirical as a source of value. For the Christian, no body of knowledge or method of investigation has cornered ultimate reality. Even using the best method of investigation, researchers still see natural, social, and supernatural things as through a mirror darkly. Yet Christians are confident the research path will loom brighter and brighter toward the perfect day (1 Cor. 13:14).

This chapter answered the question of whether Christianity and sociology converge or if they are in conflict. Clearly, the discipline is too complex in its varied theoretical perspectives to allow for a simple yes or no answer to this question. Sociology and Christianity share areas of both agreement and disagreement, and the major sociological paradigms—structural functionalism and the conflict perspective on one hand, and symbolic interactionism on the other—both confirm and disconfirm the worldview claims of Christianity.

Therefore, the key to finding balance in thinking Christianly about sociology and sociologically about Christianity is to avoid the tendency to overextend the logic of either worldview. While much of the social world, in fact, is a human construction, Christians need to resist vigorously the temptation to view all things, including God, as a social construction. On the other hand, while Christians rally to defend their belief in a transcendent, "non man-made" reality, they must not blind themselves to the reality of socially constructed phenomena. Indeed, it is in seeking balance in a holistic viewing of sociological and religious phenomena that we will be able to approach the truth of their relational unity.

References

Ashley, D., & Orenstein, D. M. (2005). *Sociological theory: Classical statements* (6th ed.). Boston: Pearson Education, Inc.

Berger, P. (1963). *Invitation to sociology: A humanistic perspective.* New York: Doubleday-Anchor.

Berger, P., & Luckman, T. (1966). *The social construction of reality.* New York: Doubleday.

Bierstedt, R. (1974). *Power and progress.* New York: McGraw-Hill.

Blumer, H. (1969). *Symbolic interactionism: Perspective and method.* Englewood Cliffs, NJ: Prentice-Hall.

Charon, J. M. (1999). *The meaning of sociology* (6th ed.). Upper Saddle River, NJ: Prentice Hall.

Comte, A. (1855). *The positive philosophy* (H. Martineau, Trans.). New York: Calvin Blanchard. (Original work published 1855)

Coser, L. A. (1977). Masters of sociological thought: Ideas in historical and social context (2nd ed.). New York: Harcourt Brace Jovanovich, Inc.

Durkheim, E. (1915). *The elementary forms of the religious life* (J. W. Swain, Trans.). London: George Allen and Unwin, 446.

Mannheim, K. (1936). *Ideology and utopia: An introduction to the sociology of knowledge* (L. Wirth & E. Shils, Trans.). New York: Harcourt, Brace & World. (Original work published 1936)

Marx, K. (1964). *Selected writings in sociology and social philosophy* (T. B. Bottomore, Trans.). London: McGraw-Hill.

Mead, G. H. (1934). *Mind, self, and society*. C.W. Morris (Ed.). Chicago: University of Chicago Press.

Migliazzo, A. C. (1993). The challenge of educational wholeness: Linking beliefs, values and academics. *Faculty Dialogue, 19*, 43–63.

Mills, C. W. (1959). *The sociological imagination*. New York: Oxford University Press.

Moberg, D. (1962). Cultural relativity and Christian faith. *Journal of the American Scientific Affiliation, 6,* 34–48.

Perkins, P. (1987). *Looking both ways: Exploring the inter-face between Christianity and sociology*. Grand Rapids, MI: Baker Book House.

Poloma, M. (1980). Theoretical models of person in contemporary sociology: Toward Christian sociological theory. In C. P. DeSanto, C. Redekop, & W. Smith-Hinds (Eds.), *A reader in sociology: Christian perspectives*. Scottsdale: Herald, 199–215.

Popper, K. (1963). Problems of scientific knowledge. *Bulletin of the International House of Japan, 12,* 12–22.

Rawls, A. W. (2004). *Epistemology and practice: Durkheim's the elementary forms of religious life*. New York: Cambridge University Press.

Rawls, A. W. (1996). Durkheim's epistemology: The neglected argument. *American Journal of Sociology, 102*(2), 430–482.

Ritzer, G. (1988). *Contemporary sociological theory* (2nd ed.). New York: Alfred A. Knopf.

Scheler, M. (1980). *Problems of a sociology of knowledge* (M. Frings, Trans.). K. Stikkers (Ed.). London: Routledge & Kegan Paul.

Schwalbe, M. (2001). *The sociologically examined life: Pieces of the conversation* (2nd ed.). Mountain View, CA: Mayfield Publishing Company.

Steinmetz, G. (2004, September). Odious comparisons: Incommensurability, the case study, and "small n's" in sociology. *Sociological Theory,*

22(3), 371–400.

Tibbetts, P. (1982). The Positivism-Humanism Debate in Sociology: A Reconsideration. *Sociological Inquiry*, *52*(3), 184-199.

Weber, Max (1946). *From Max Weber: Essays in sociology* (H. Gerth & C. W. Mills, Trans.). London: Oxford.

Weber, M. (1949). *The methodology of the social sciences* (E. A. Shils & H. A. Finch, Trans.). Glencoe, IL, Free Press.

Weber, M. (1958). Wissenschaft als Beruf, Gesammelte Aufsaetze zur Wissenschaftslebre, Tübingen, 1922 [Science as a Vocation]. In H. Gerth & C. Wright Mills (Eds.), *Essays in Sociology* (pp. 129–56). Oxford: Houghton Mifflin Company.

White, E. (1888). *The great controversy*. Mountain View, CA: Pacific Press Publishing Association.

Zeitlin, I. M. (2001). *Ideology and the development of sociological theory* (7th ed.). Upper Saddle, NJ: Prentice-Hall, Inc.

CHAPTER THREE

THE CHURCH AND THE SOCIOLOGICAL CONNECTION

This chapter makes the claim that the church is both social and spiritual. It discusses the developmental and operational patterns of the Adventist church as a function of social forces. Moberg's model of the life cycle of a church is used to examine the extent to which the Seventh-day Adventist church conforms to a predictable pattern. The evolution of the doctrinal tenets and the institutional network that currently serve the church are addressed.

The church is a social organism as well as a divinely originated and sustained phenomenon, a product of both social conditioning and divine intervention. The spiritual and the social, as these exist in the human context, are not mutually exclusive entities; they are, in fact, integrally related one to the other. While it must be admitted that God, the ultimate essence of the spiritual, transcends the social and therefore exists independent of the social as a being, within the human context He remains hidden and meaningless in the absence of social interaction. Indeed, without a grounding in the social, God would be muted and isolated from humans.

This is the lesson to be grasped from the incarnation—God assuming human form and taking up lodgment within the human system so that He could more effectively communicate and demonstrate His love for humans. It seems that no interaction of substance can exist between the Infinite (God) and the finite (humans), the Absolute and the relative, without some accommodation on the part of God. Accordingly, Van Bemmelen (1998) conceives of the incarnation as a sort of Divine accommodation in which God adjusts Himself to the mental and spiritual capacity of humans so that they can know Him, trust Him, and love Him. Without the entry of God into human community, it would be difficult to realize ideas of Him and a relationship with Him.

The Divine's embrace of the social stands in contrast to the dualistic and dichotomous posture some Christians have assumed toward life. But this Cartesian block[1] must be overcome if Christians are to demonstrate consistency in their creedal beliefs and social practice. In this way they provide proof of the relevance of their faith and give notice of their acceptance of life as a holistic process. To ignore such a holism is to deny the demonstration of the incarnation and court the indictment of critics.

Karl Marx (1859, p. 44) leveled such a criticism in his characterization of religion as the "opium of the people." He pointed out that religious consciousness is false consciousness because of the disconnect it allows between the material and the nonmaterial worlds. Though Marx's basic argument is of course much more embedded in his historical-materialist philosophical musings about the question of being, the rigid dichotomy some have imposed between religion and the rest of the world provides ample basis for his contention.

The incarnation of Christ speaks eloquently to the bridging of the empirical (material) and the non-empirical (spiritual). As John (1:14) indicates, Jesus (the Word) became flesh so that we might see the truth of His glory. Through the incarnation (the divine embracing humanity) we are no more alienated, and in our "earthiness" we have become sons and daughters of (and one with) God (Eph. 2:19). Indeed, the incarnation underscores the point that God has implemented, and intends to bring to fruition, His plan for our restoration in Him, within the human context. Of course, He could have accomplished this task merely by speaking from a distance. However, He came and performed in human form, thereby demonstrating His supreme regard for the human context as the medium for His redemptive outreach to humankind.

The incarnation must, therefore, be the touchstone by which discussions of the operation of God's kingdom on earth (the church) are rationalized. In this connection, the whole process of the Divine accommodation becomes instructive, particularly Jesus' own socialization experience, His personal development, and His interactional style. It is on the basis of the lessons drawn from these that it is safe to draw conclusions about the proper role and constitution of the church.

The holistic development of Jesus' socialization experience is clear in the record of St. Luke, who reports that Jesus developed in wisdom (intellectually) and stature (physically) and in favor with God (spiritually) and

---

1. This construct draws on Descartes's dualism of mind and body and suggests that an embrace of such dualism impedes our capacity to truly grasp reality as it is.

men (socially) (Luke 1:52). This profile suggests the kind of operational model the church should embrace in its attempt to facilitate wholeness in Jesus.

Fraser and Campolo (1992), accordingly, challenge us to keep religion connected to the rest of life. These Christian sociologists argue that the "Christian faith cannot accept the division between the public and the private, the sacred and the secular, science and faith, facts and values..." since, as they point out, "Jesus is Lord of all creation, all peoples, all history and all dimensions of human experience" (p. 43). These loaded statements must be read carefully and accepted in the spirit in which they were written. The idea advanced here is not that all realities become fused or that no distinction exists between given categories and phenomena, but rather that Christians ought to be sensitive and relate to all aspects of life as interconnected pieces. To embrace such a position is to be logically sociological; it is to refuse to isolate the particular as such and emphasize the general as a predictor of the particular. In other words, to view life as a composite of interconnected pieces is to recognize the principle of interdependence and to appreciate the extent to which the particular is an outcome of the general. Indeed, it is to take on the sociological perspective.

The extent to which Seventh-day Adventism bears a sociological connection must be grasped if the ongoing operations (current and historical) of this socio-religious organism are to be truly appreciated. This is not meant in terms of the empiricist claim of the discipline, that is, that reality is ultimately sensory and is to be grasped as such. Adventists are idealists in the sense that they believe that the nonempirical is primary and therefore constitutes the basis of the empirical (the material). This position agrees with the Apostle Paul's suggestion that the things that are seen derive from things that are not seen (2 Cor. 4:18).[2]

The philosophy and practice orientation of Seventh-day Adventism reflect an acknowledgment of and commitment to the holistic nature of life. Specifically, judged in the light of its fundamental beliefs and corporate practices, Seventh-day Adventism can be said to be responsive to social

2. This text may be more fruitfully rendered in the context of our discussion as follows: Things that are not empirical (not grasped through the senses) predate and will survive things that are empirical (things grasped through the senses). Things empirical are not eternal and thus are not fundamental and durable but temporal, arising from things that are non-empirical (things not within the realm of the sensory).

forces. However, despite the recognition conceded in previous works (Bull & Lockhart, 1989; Dudley & Hernandez, 1992; Knight, 2000; Land, 1986) to the socio-structural connection of the church, sociology still languishes for due appreciation within the church. Misconceptions regarding its value to the church and society in general are all too common, and the discipline is yet to be fully appreciated by college students. Not only within Christian colleges in general (and it seems much more so in Seventh-day Adventist colleges) but also within secular institutions of higher learning, sociology is yet to command the attention it deserves.

While this smothered interest in sociology may be attributed to the tendency of sociologists to "deconstruct"[3] human behavior and society, laying bare the social nature of such behaviors, it may also be placed upon the failure of Christian sociologists to demonstrate the value of the discipline in an appealing and sustained fashion. In order to make good on the latter, Christian sociologists must demonstrate supportive linkages between sociology and issues of faith. They must be able to show how the sociological perspectives aid in a deeper and broader understanding of the Christian life. They may accomplish this by employing sociological methods and theories to shed light upon and predict various empirical patterns within the church through various research projects.

Many issues of relevance to the Christian life and role in society continue to confront Christians: marital conflict, marital quality and stability, divorce, drug addiction, spiritual development, factors that predict church growth, and factors that predict church/pastor cordiality. Christian sociologists who employ their sociological insights and skills to shed light upon such issues fulfill a useful function; they also advance the cause of sociology.

Social Forces Impact the Development of Adventism

Despite their belief that they were raised up by God to advance the promulgation of the Three Angels' Messages of Revelation 14, Seventh-day Adventists bear no illusion as to the social conditions that shaped and continue to influence the emergence and operation of their denomination. Land (1986), a noted Adventist historian, suggests that Seventh-day Adventism, like other denominations such as the Jehovah's Witnesses and

---

3. This is politically a radical position on human conduct, and it flies in the face of the more conservative individualist argument, which places the thrust of human behavior in personal individual characteristics rather than forces external to them.

the Latter-day Saints, emerged out of the social and religious turmoil of the mid-nineteenth century (p. vii). Bull and Lockhart (1989) conclude that Seventh-day Adventism, with its current theological and structural posture, is largely a reaction to American civil religion, while Dudley and Hernandez (1992) suggest that Seventh-day Adventists are citizens of two worlds, i.e., they embrace both secular and religious mores in their individual lives.

Certainly, these observations do not imply that the church is exclusively tied to the social milieu, but they do serve to highlight the relevance of the sociological perspective to an understanding of the development of the church. If indeed socio-historical factors undergird the emergence of Seventh-day Adventism, then it is within those circumstances that one must seek to locate explanations of the dynamics of this socio-religious organism.

The rise, emergence, and continued operations of Seventh-day Adventism can be seen to be informed by sociological factors, the extent of which may be traced to the following: (1) the varied institutional forms and practice orientation of this religious body over time, (2) the dynamic nature of its teachings, and (3) the centrality of the operation of various social organizations to its overall culture and mission. An understanding of these aspects of Seventh-day Adventism will lend to a greater appreciation of the church's sociological connection.

Institutional and Practice Orientation of Seventh-day Adventism over Time

From its formative years, the Seventh-day Adventist church has had to contend with social pressures that mediated its evolving patterns and rate of development. For example, Anderson (1986) identified and discussed some of the pertinent tensions that stymied early efforts at formal organization in the Seventh-day Adventist church, tracing these tensions to the negative attitude of members toward the secular political system. He observed that the negative attitude of church members toward state organizations reproduced itself in their opposition toward the church's own attempts at formal organization. Several factors may have conditioned this response. *Organizing to Beat the Devil: The Development of Adventist Church Structure*, George Knight's (2001) account of how the Seventh-day Adventist church became organized, alludes to several such factors. Among the predisposing contexts he identifies are the Connexionist Movement and reactions to the ill-fated Millerite vision.[4]

The Christian Connexion proliferated in several parts of the United States during the early years of the nineteenth century. This group was not so much concerned with the establishment of set doctrines as it was "to assert, for individuals and churches, more liberty and independence in relation to matters of faith and practice, to shake up the authority of human creeds and the shackles of prescribed modes and forms; to make the Bible their only guide…" (Knight, 2001, p. 15). Not surprisingly, those who embraced these ideas were skeptical of organized religion. Expectedly, members of the Christian Connexion perceived formal organization as being of the devil.

Since many of those who constituted the early Seventh-day Adventist movement had previously embraced Connexionist ideas, including prominent leaders Joseph Bates and James White, the resistance that greeted efforts to organize formally in the early years of the church should not be too difficult to appreciate. Many viewed efforts to organize as devilish and "Babylonian." In fact, George Storr, one of the intellectuals of the young religious movement, argued that "no church can be organized by man's invention but what it becomes Babylon the moment it is organized" (Knight, 2001, p. 23). The impact of Connexionist thought on Seventh-day Adventism was such that the early years of the 1850s saw what was nearly a replica of the organizational structure of the Christian Connexion.

On the other hand, the recognition of a need for plans to arrest the sagging hope and continued splintering of this ex-Millerite movement proved fairly successful. Implementation of these plans brought a rapid increase in membership in the young church. This, as well as the expanded vision of mission embraced by its leaders, created an awareness of the need for better structure. This felt need for structure paved the way for a more benign view of organization in the young church. Thus the need to move beyond a loosely organized Connexionist model of church order was embraced. Knight (2001) suggests that this need was deepened by the church's awareness that ethical and doctrinal unity needed to be sustained. Thus, concerns

---

4. William Miller interpreted the cleansing of the sanctuary in Daniel 7 to mean that Jesus would return to the earth on the 22nd of October, 1844, and warned the early Advent believers to prepare for the occasion. The non-occurrence of this event created dismay among the ranks.

and plans for a more predictable pattern of governance led to the legal establishment of the church in 1863.

Seventh-day Adventism: A Predictable Cycle?

Moberg's (1962) life cycle of a church provides the basic framework for this analysis. In his discussion of the church as a social institution, this Christian sociologist agrees with Blumer (1955) that as institutions develop they generate informal and formal structures in the forms of traditions, values, norms, goals, policies, and collective feelings of morale among their followers. Over time, and with the increase of membership, these structural forms are gradually modified. Informal structures tend to give way to more formal ones, with primary group relationships yielding to an ever-expanding bureaucracy.

Both Max Weber and Robert Michels identified this tendency for institutions to become less people-centered and more rule-driven as they increased in size and structure. Michels talks of the "iron law of oligarchy" in which the institutional mind of an elite few comes to dominate the will of the many, while Weber identifies the relentless march of society's rational approach, leading to an "iron cage" of instrumentality, where there are "specialists without spirit and sensualists without heart" (cited in Elwell, 1996, p. 19).

Moberg (1962) contends that while institutional bureaucracy often leads to efficiency, a vicious cycle tends to develop in which increasing formalization may lead to impaired effectiveness. Applying this line of reasoning to the church, he suggests that the sociological forces attendant upon the development of the institutional church predispose it to certain predictable trajectories. He has accordingly identified five stages that characterize the natural history of a church: incipient organization, formal organization, maximum efficiency, institutionalism, and disintegration.

Knight (1991) has argued that the Seventh-day Adventist developmental pattern fits into the general life cycle of a church as identified by Moberg. He is quick to point out, however, that the application of Moberg's model to the Seventh-day Adventist church does not suggest that sociological patterns necessarily predetermine everything about the church. While he is convinced that the model sheds much light on the development and current status of Adventism, he notes that there is not a perfect correlation.

The first stage in the history of the institutional church is generally characterized by sorting tension. It is the time when dissatisfaction with existing structures generates much conflict and unrest. This tension often leads to the emergence of a new cult or sect with identifiable characteristics. There is usually a high degree of collective excitement, "unplanned and uncontrollable emotions," accompanied by bodily possession by the Holy Spirit. It is during this stage that "charismatic, authoritarian, and prophetic" leaders tend to emerge (Moberg, 1962, p. 119).

For Knight (1991), the Adventist church paralleled Moberg's stage of incipient development during the years 1844 to 1863. It was during this period that the seminal group of the current Seventh-day Adventist church came into existence. Two factors seem especially pertinent to this event: the rejection of Miller's teaching by other religious groups and the refusal of some disenchanted Millerites to accept the Sabbath and the ministration of Christ in the heavenly sanctuary.

During these early years, the church was led by Joseph Bates, James White, and Ellen White—people whose leadership could be described respectively as charismatic, authoritarian, and prophetic. In those early days in the life of the church, little emphasis was placed on structure as a source of stability; rather, early church leaders felt that the active presence of the Holy Spirit, indicated through visions and healings, should be relied upon for the needed guidance.

Seventh-day Adventism, according to Knight, entered Moberg's second life cycle stage at about 1863 and peaked at this developmental stage around 1901. During this period, several patterns in the Seventh-day Adventist church conformed with the characteristics of the second stage of Moberg's natural history cycle (see Table 3.1). Emphasis was placed on the need for organization, unlike the previous stage when to be organized was perceived as a step toward "Babylon." Church leaders also recognized the need to develop a separate corporate culture supported by a core of doctrinal beliefs. This led, among other things, to the organization in 1863 of the General Conference, the highest-ranking body of the Seventh-day Adventist church. It was also during this period of formal organization that a lifestyle agenda was set and the foundation for the current supporting institutional network was laid. For example, during this time, Ellen White propounded the health principles that were to become the bedrock of Adventists' health practices. Additionally, during these years the denomination declared its non-combatancy policy and also advanced guidelines on matters of dress and adornment. The establishment of the church's first medical, educational, and publishing institutions all emerged during this stage. The crystallization and promulgation of the church's doctrinal positions also marked this stage.

Table 3.1
A Summary of Moberg's Life Cycle of Religious Organizations

Stages	Characteristics
Incipient Organization	1. Dissatisfaction with existing churches 2. Reaction against departure from traditional folkways and mores 3. Emergence of a cult or sect when leadership of the "dissatisfied" arises 4. Emerging sects have a high degree of collective excitement and new belief that subject it to the suspicion of insanity 5. Leadership is so diffused that a founder is hard to designate
Formal Organization	1. Complete separation from the parental church 2. Goals are formulated and publicized to attract additional members 3. Symbolic expressions (i.e., no jewelry, alcohol, or dancing) of differences between the new church and the worldly non-members 4. Codes of behavior are developed and enforced 5. Agitational forms of leadership gradually diminish
Maximum Efficiency	1. Less emotionalism and dominance by statesmen 2. Rationalism replaces charismatic leadership 3. Historians and apologists emerge 4. Institution at a stage of maximum vitality and rapid growth 5. Internal dissension may lead to the rise of splinter groups or disintegration of the sect

Stages	Characteristics
Institutionalism	1. The church has become a bureaucracy
	2. Organized worship becomes a ritual
	3. Conflict with "the world" is replaced by toleration
	4. Sermons digress from church dogma to social issues and topical lectures
	5. Membership becomes passive and remote from leadership
Disintegration	1. Red tape, absolutism, and corruption set in
	2. Constituents lose confidence because the institutional machine lacks responsiveness to personal and social needs

Adapted from Moberg (1962)

However, by the end of the nineteenth century, the growth in membership both nationally and internationally rendered the church's 1863 organizational model inadequate. This need for reorganization ushered the church into Moberg's third developmental stage of maximum efficiency. During the 1901 General Conference session, the establishment of union conferences and the departmental structure that continue to operate at all levels of the church today were voted into action. Apart from these historic decisions, the election of the statesman—like A. G. Daniells to the General Conference presidency—and the broadening of the church's educational vision in the creation of two universities (all these taking place in the latter half of the 1950s and the early 1960s) signaled that the Seventh-day Adventist church had arrived at the maximum efficiency stage (Knight, 1991).

The fourth stage of the natural history of churches is institutionalism. One of the characteristics of this stage is formalism in which emphasis is given to procedures and rules. Another characteristic is the domination of the church bureaucracy by leaders who give much attention to maintaining established patterns, sometimes at the expense of promoting the otherworldly goals that gave the church its identity. This leads to the line of distinctiveness between the church and the "world" becoming blurred, as the bureaucracy seeks a respectable and nonthreatening status in its host society. A liberal and rational approach to life is embraced, and activities and ideas once deemed worldly and sinful lose their hideousness and become major attractions.

In spite of Knight's conclusion that the Seventh-day Adventist church had not yet reached Moberg's fourth or fifth stage, some evidence seems to indicate an approximation of these stages. For example, the high level of tension that characterized the relationship between the Seventh-day Adventist church and the host society during the early decades of its existence had subsided considerably by the 1980s. Lawson (1996) argues this position on at least three counts.

He points to the erosion of the church's position on non-combatancy, that is, its refusal to bear arms in the event of a war. Lawson observes that the church's position shifted from non-combatancy in World War I, to "conscientious cooperators in World War II, and not to passing judgment on those who bear arms" during the Vietnam War (p. 50). He notes that during the Gulf War in 1991, between 6,000 and 8,000 Adventists enlisted, with 2,000 actually participating.

A second area identified relates to the principle of the separation of church and State. Initially the church sought to maintain this relationship by not accepting funds from the government. However, Lawson notes that by 1972 the church had relented from this position and agreed to accept funding for its educational institutions with the understanding that financial aid from the government would not require the church to surrender its right to teach its religious principles.

Yet another factor that signaled a decrease of tension between the church and its host society rests with the church's desire to improve its public image by gaining acceptance and respect from the host society. For example, Lawson (1996) observes that when schismatic Adventist groups in the USSR and Hungary proved an irritant to political leaders, the ranking church official intervened in both instances, giving his blessing to the element of the church that showed a willingness to comply with the State. Subsequently, the church "cemented a close relationship...with the chair of the USSR Council on religious affairs," paving the way for the church to receive approval for the creation of an Adventist seminary in Russia (p. 51).

Churches outside of the United States of America courted the favor of the State. All this was possible because, Lawson argues, "a policy of pursuing reduced tension with the governments emerged and eventually flourished within Adventism" (p. 52). Of course, these trends do not necessarily suggest that the church has abdicated its foundational principles of operation, but only that it has pursued a policy of détente with the host society. Though these examples do not match all of the characteristics of Moberg's fourth stage, it is clear that some of the qualities are present. In particular, policy aimed at reducing tension between the church and its host society not only generated harmony but also paved the way for a blurring of the line of distinctiveness between the church's operation and the surrounding society. The church might have approached Moberg's fifth stage, disintegration, during the 1990s when a number of congregations, for one reason or another, defected from the church and formed their own independent ministries.

The degree to which one may fruitfully apply Moberg's natural history typology to a sociological account of the Seventh-day Adventist church is by no means a simple determination. For one thing, Seventh-day Adventism today has grown rather complex in its ethnic, national, class, and ideological diversity. Hence, its emerging patterns defy a simple, monolithic linear account. If one looks closely enough, characteristics of each of the life cycle stages can be detected in different regional and national situations. In some parts of the United States, the church may have run the full gamut of the cycle; in other places, both in the United States and beyond its borders, the church may yet be proceeding at earlier stages of the cycle. What is of value in our discussion here, however, is the demonstration that the organizational character and outlook of the church tend to approximate Moberg's predictable sociological patterns. To the extent that this is so, the position that the church is responsive to sociological forces is reinforced.

Anomalies within the Church

It is against the understanding that sociological factors constrain patterns within the church that we may grasp "anomalies"[5] between ideal and real values in the church's operation. Because of sin and its impact on the mediating social structure, the church has not always succeeded in its operations in aligning its practice with its ideals. For example, the belief that everyone is equal in the eyes of God may coexist side by side with unequal treatment toward some groups of people within the church. Also a fervent

---

5. In this context, anomalies are any concept, event, or behavioral content that does not line up with the prescribed (ideal) norm of a social system.

belief and yearning for unity may be paralleled by the institutionalization and perpetuation of structures that promote disunity. A value/practice deficit[6] may thus develop in which social practice lags behind embraced values in the church, giving rise to questions about the role of God in all of this. Anomalies such as sexism, racism, tribalism, and nationalism have surfaced within the church from time to time. When this happens, people tend either to dismiss the church as not being under the guidance of God or to react with the type of resignation that says "God will fix it in His own time." Seldom are the explanations sought within the associated circumstances in which the church operates; yet therein may lie the answer to the questions that arise.

Let us take a look at the issue of sexism, for example. Sexism is the belief that one sex, or gender, is naturally superior to the other and therefore is better suited for and entitled to certain roles than the other. In particular, it has been proposed that women are naturally deficient and weaker in nature than men. Thomas Aquinas was convinced that women's chief role was childbearing and that they could not be of much help to men otherwise (Watts, 1995).

Those sentiments were rife in the early years of the nineteenth century, when Adventism was taking root in the American culture. During that time, women enjoyed few rights and were in fact treated as children and slaves. They could not own property or have any legal say about their children independent of their husbands (Henslin, 2004). These Victorian views of women, Daily (1985) argues, did not escape the views and policy orientation of the developing Adventist church. He observes, for example, that the notion of "vitalism" promoted by Ellen White was already in vogue when she advanced it to the young church. "Ellen White," Daily notes, "had been deeply influenced by Horace Mann and L. B. Coles" (p. 101), the latter being a physician who had definite leanings towards vitalism. Thus, White wrote in 1864 that "females possess less vital force than the other sex..." (Daily, 1985, p. 11). Hence, White's position on women's participation in public ministry was rather conservative as it accorded much with nineteenth-century beliefs about women's role in society.

However, research led Watts (1995) to conclude that Ellen White gradually became more emphatic about women's role in public ministry,

___

6. In the sociological literature this term is conceptualized in terms of ideal culture versus real culture.

to the point where White expressly stated that when women "consecrate themselves to God...they are just as verily laborers for God as are their husbands" (White, 1898). Though Ellen White in this reference does not intend a focus on public pastoral work, it does seem to indicate a more benign view of womens' role in the gospel ministry. Indeed, the progressive revelation principle of Scripture is also true for the prophetess: "the path of the just is as a shining light that shineth more and more into the perfect day" (Prov. 4:18).

In this light, it is all the more understandable that the church's position had varied regarding women's participation in the gospel ministry as well as their meaningful involvement in other areas of denominational work. The question of giving full ministerial rights (with ordination) to women is still being debated with, it seems, a widening divergence of opinions on the issue. Those who stoutly oppose the full integration of women into the gospel ministry justify their position on the ground that the Bible does not support such integration. Those who reject this claim draw attention to the varying pattern of women's involvement in denominational work over time.

Watts (1995) observes that prior to Ellen White's death in 1915, women were employed in several positions of responsibility, at various levels of the church, including the General Conference. But that quickly changed in the decades after her death. For example, women held more than 33 percent of Conference treasury positions in 1905, but by 1945 no women were to be found in those positions. Also, while in 1905 about 50 percent of Conference secretaries were women, by 1937 that number had dwindled to 0 percent. These patterns, and related ones, were not attributable to new light received on women's participation; rather, as several scholars have noted, this was the result of policy changes occasioned by socio-economic trends (Dasher, 1992; Haloviak, 1990; Pearson, 1990).

Doctrinal Development and Social Forces

If there is but a single aspect of the development of Seventh-day Adventism that those who share a belief in the divine guidance of this religious body are not likely to attribute to the impact of social forces, it is the corpus of its doctrines that have evolved over time. Yet evidence exists to the contrary that even this sensitive, Spirit-guided area of the church's life does not transcend the influence of the social. One thing seems certain: the set of teachings that currently constitute the fundamental beliefs of the church would not have found ready acceptance with the founding members. In some instances, the founders of Adventism would have viewed these core beliefs as unbiblical and false. Current teachings on the Trinity would have been opposed by most early Adventist leaders (Gane, 1963; Moon, 2003). James White, one of the pioneers of the Adventist church, alluded to the idea of the Trinity as that "old unscriptural trinitarian creed" (Moon, 2003, p. 1). Bates (1868), another pioneer, saw the said idea as equally unbiblical. Moon (2003) suggests that Jesus was not viewed by the early Adventists as co-eternal and identical with God the Father. Further, the Holy Spirit was considered to be just an influence (Bates, 1868; Moon, 2003), not a full bodily member of the Godhead as is now believed.

Knight (2000) suggests that the positions held by Bates and White on the Trinity are attributable to the Restorationist background of these two Adventist pioneers. He also noted that other doctrinal stances of the early Adventist church such as the rejection of creeds and the restoration of the Sabbath, especially promoted by Bates, were Restorationist emphases as well.

Ellen White too would have found herself in some opposition to the current doctrinal position of the church she helped to found. Early in her ministry she embraced the view that the Sabbath starts at 6 P.M. on Friday and ends at 6 P.M. on Saturday, contrary to the evening-to-evening position of the Bible currently espoused by the church (Knight, 2000). Additionally, "it is entirely plausible" that Ellen White "grew in her understanding of the Godhead" (Moon, 2003, p. 2), though it is not specified in what aspect she might have.

Guy (2002) underscores the staggered process that marked the evolving of the fundamental beliefs of Adventism. In his efforts to uncover the origins of the fundamental beliefs embraced by Adventists, Guy traces the various attempts made at constituting a doctrinal core that would earn wide acceptance. The process spans a long period of time, beginning in 1853 and gaining momentum at various junctures in 1854, 1864, 1872, 1894, and 1931 when various statements were advanced. These attempts were not without the opposition of those who saw them as movements towards the establishment of a creed.

However, at the 1980 General Conference (GC) session, twenty-seven fundamental beliefs were adopted. These were later extended at the 2005 GC session to include a twenty-eighth fundamental belief. Clearly, an evolving pattern in doctrinal beliefs is evident. Yet this should be no surprise, given the observation of Ellen White (1948): "Whenever the people of God are growing in grace, they will be constantly obtaining a clearer understanding of His Word. They will discern new light and beauty in its sacred truths. This has been true in the history of the church in all ages, and thus it will continue to the end" (p. 11).

Moreover, what stands out is the possibility that members may conceptualize, and indeed have conceptualized, the fundamentals differently. This follows from the fact that people are not the same across the board, given their cultural and social frames of references. Accordingly, Guy (2002) has argued that "Adventists are not all alike, and so Adventist theology is not exactly alike. It can't be, and we shouldn't imagine that it can" (p. 14).

Yet, past and current variations in what and how Adventists believed and believe are not indicative of the relativity of truth but rather of the progressive and dynamic nature of the unfolding of truth (Guy, 2002; White, 1948). This progressive and dynamic character of the revelation of truth is informed not by the inability of the author of truth (God) to dispense it all at once. Rather, it is attributable to the limited capacity of humans to take it in as truth. Thus, in light of their becoming like God, humans are in process and will always be in process. This is so because God is infinite, and the human context through which He seeks to communicate His mind to humans is limited and ever evolving. It also seems that God seizes the advantageous flow of the human context—given time, place, and circumstance—to maximize the effectiveness of the communicated content. He reveals Himself to us patiently, awaiting the favorable moment to press home His significant point. Within this perspective, the emergent nature of the fundamental beliefs of the Seventh-day Adventist church becomes plausible and meaningful.

Adventism and Social Institutions

The fact that communities and nations are sustained centrally by social patterns and the associated network of social institutions underscores the value of social institutions. The institutions of the family, education, the economy, and government are thus indispensable to the well being and stability of communities and nations. Through these institutions, a nation socializes its citizens, teaches them values and skills, systematically meets their needs for goods and services, and guarantees them a sense of security through the maintenance of order. Society is thus explainable by its social institutions.

Notwithstanding its avowed reliance on divine guidance, the Seventh-day Adventist church, because of its holistic philosophy, is likewise dependent upon social institutions for its well being and sustenance. The appreciation of this need surfaced as the church grew. Its leaders, faced with the need for expanding and deepening the organizational structure, passed measures toward this effect at the historic 1901 GC Session. The foundation policies of the church's current structure and its educational, medical, and publishing institutions were framed at that session and in the post-session period.

The network of institutions that sustain the Adventist church grew to the point that Milton Yinger (1970), in his typology of religious organizations, classified Seventh-day Adventism among the most highly structured (bureaucratized) church organizations. This proliferation and deepening of the institutional cluster highlights the value the Seventh-day Adventist church places on social institutions as vehicles of continuity and change.

Ellen White was especially strong in her advocacy of the family, education, and medical institutions as channels of Christian development. She saw the work of education and redemption as identical (White, 1903), characterizing education as more than the pursuit of a course of study but as a preparation for the joys of service in this world and the next as well. While she saw the family as the foundation of the church and society, she perceived the medical work as the right arm of Adventism.

The church's investments in the educational, familial, and medical institutions attest to the role they play in the life of the church. Seventh-day Adventism places special emphasis on the education institution. As of July 2005, the church operated 5,300 elementary schools, 1,320 secondary schools, and one hundred colleges and universities across the world (http://www.adventist.org/world_church/facts_and_figures/index. html.en). Humberto Rasi, former worldwide education director of the Seventh-day Adventist church, observes in the same newsletter that God created humans as integrated units of body, mind, and spirit and that students learn how to make decisions on the basis of inculcated moral principles and permanent values. By facilitating the teaching and internalization of social values and moral principles, the educational institution reinforces the philosophy of the church and orients beneficiaries towards God (GC Bulletin, 2000 #5).

In terms of medical institutions, as of December 2004, the church operated 167 hospitals and sanitariums, 407 clinics and dispensaries, 124 nursing homes, and attended to over 13,000,000 outpatient visits (http://www.adventist.org/world_church/facts_and_figures/index.html.en). While these institutional units facilitate physical and mental well being, they are operated under the philosophy that an intimate connection exists between physical, mental, and spiritual well being.

Seventh-day Adventists believe that the family is the primary setting in which Christian values are processed and internalized across generations and that the nature of our family relationships profoundly impact our capacity for love and intimacy with other people and God (Flowers, in GC Bulletin, 2000 # 8). Therefore, the church has set up family life departments at each organizational level of its operation. These departments spearhead the production of family-friendly resources, plan and implement marriage and family enrichment workshops/seminars, and encourage scientific research on family values. The general view is that effective and enriched families make for a more effective and enriched church and thus promote spiritual growth.

Does the Process of Social Determinism Negate the Possibility of Divine Intervention?

This discussion has sought to demonstrate that the church, though a divinely-guided entity, is integrally social. Unfortunately, the latter claim has been the source of concern to some Christians, for whom a sociological account of religious phenomena explains away the role of divine guidance. The supporting logic seems to be that since God's ways are not our ways and He (God) is past finding out, His role in the life and society of humans cannot be captured by human (social) means. But this is a careless position, taking Scripture out of context.

More fundamentally, such a view of the Divine Reality flows from a dualistic understanding of the world. Two worlds are assumed to exist: "a natural realm of human events and a supernatural realm" (Clarke & Gaede, 1987, p. 72). Within this dualism, God's participation in human life and society are framed in the mysterious and miraculous, and as such are beyond empirical investigation. The human realm, on the other hand, stands bereft of the divine and so may be captured through the empirical.

However, this dichotomous treatment of reality not only denies God's ongoing participation in nature and human systems, but it also ignores the lesson of the incarnation. Indeed, the God of Scripture is not only transcendent but also immanent. He supersedes all that is natural and man-made but remains actively involved in both. The Apostle Paul records that He is not far away (Acts 17:27) and that in Him we live and move and have our being (Acts 17:28).

Further, the denial that divine intervention is empirically detectable and can be studied as such sounds disturbingly agnostic. But the agnostic's claim that God is not knowable stands opposed to the very words of the incarnated Jesus, who said, "I know my sheep (followers) and I am known by them" (John 10:14). The claim also opposes Jesus' promise that His followers will be made free by the knowledge of the truth (John 8:32). Additionally, Jesus' response to Philip, who requested that the disciples be shown the Father (i.e., God the Father), resonates with the notion that truth is not only spiritual but empirical as well. Jesus remarked to Philip that if they have seen Him (the incarnated, in-the-flesh Jesus) they have seen the Father (John 14:8). Finally, Paul supports the claim that God is empirically knowable. Since the creation of the world, he says, God's invisible (non-empirical) qualities—His eternal power and divine nature—have been clearly seen, being understood from what has been made (the empirical) (Rom. 1:20).

Hence, to position the church within the realm of the social is not to deny its divine nature. Further, to argue that the church in its operation is informed by social forces does not constitute an attempt to obscure the true source of its empowerment, Jesus. Indeed, the church is the visible expression of the God-man, Jesus, who through His incarnation has legitimized the integration of the spiritual and the social. Therefore, attempts to place the human and the Divine, the social and the spiritual, in opposition to each other take away from the holistic nature of the spiritual. Such attempts undermine efforts aimed at knowing God through the varied range of the human experience.

All this, of course, does not mean that the human is identical with the Divine or that the Divine can be exhaustively captured in human terms. What it does suggest, however, is that it is not possible to make sense of the Divine in our midst apart from terms and circumstances by which meaning is arrived at in the human context. And it is the role of Christian sociologists to reverently uphold this to their students.

References

Anderson, G. T. (1986). Sectarianism and organization. In G. Land (Ed.), *Adventism in America*. Grand Rapids, MI: Eerdmans Publishing Co.

Bates, J. (1868). *The autobiography of elder Joseph Bates*. Battle Creek, MI: SDA Publishing, 205.

Blumer, H. G. (1955). Social movements. In Alfred M. Lee (Ed.), *Principles of sociology*. New York: Barnes and Noble.

Bull, M., & Lockhart, D. (1989). *Seeking a sanctuary: Seventh-day Adventism and the American dream*. New York: Harper & Row.

Clark, R. A., & Gaede, S. D. (1987). Knowing together: Reflections on a holistic sociology of knowledge. In H. Heie and D. L. Wolfe (Eds.), *The reality of Christian learning* (pp. 72–92). Grand Rapids, MI: Eerdmans Publishing Co.

Daily, S. G. (1985). The irony of Adventism: The role of Ellen White and other Adventist women in nineteenth century America. Dissertation presented to the School of Theology at Claremont, pp. 11, 101.

Dasher, B. (1992). Women's leadership, 1915-1970: The waning years. In R. T. Banks (Ed.), *A woman's place: Seventh-day Adventist women in church and society*. Hagerstown, MD: Review and Herald Publishing Association.

Dudley, R. L., & Hernandez, E. I. (1992). *Citizens of two worlds: Religion and politics among American Seventh-day Adventists*. Berrien Springs, MI: Andrews University Press.

Elwell, F. (1996). *The sociology of Max Weber*. Retrieved May 19, 2005, from Verstchen: Max Weber's website: http://www.faculty.rsu.edu/~felwell/Theorists/Weber/Whome.htm

Flowers, R. (2000). *General Conference Bulletin*, 5.

Flowers, R. (2000). *General Conference Bulletin*, 8.

Fraser, D. A., & Campolo, T. (1992). *Sociology through the eyes of faith*. New York: HarperCollins Publishers.

Gane, E. R. (1963). The arian or anti-trinitarian views presented in Seventh-day Adventist literature and the Ellen G. White answer. Unpublished master's thesis, Andrews University, Berrien Springs, MI.

Guy, F. (2002). Mapping the past: Exploring the development of Adventist theology. Retrieved September 1, 2005, from http://www.sdanet.org/atissue/doctrines/au2002conference/guy/guy-past.htm

Guy, F. (2002). Uncovering the origins of the statement of twenty-seven fundamental beliefs. Retrieved September 1, 2005, from http://www. sdanet.org/atissue/doctrines/au2002conference/guy/guy27origin.htm

Haloviak, B. (1990). *Adventism's lost generations: The decline of leadership positions for SDA women.* Unpublished manuscript.

Henslin, J. M. (2004). *Sociology: A down-to-earth approach* (7th ed.). Boston: Allyn and Bacon.

Knight, G. R. (1991, June). Adventism, institutionalism, and the challenge of secularization. *Ministry, 64*(6), 6–10, 29.

Knight, G. R. (2000). *A search for identity.* Hagerstown, MD: Review and Herald Publishing Association.

Knight, G. R. (2001). *Organizing to beat the devil: The development of Adventist church structure.* Hagerstown, MD: Review and Herald Publishing Association.

Land, G. (Ed.). (1986). *Adventism in America.* Grand Rapids, MI: Eerdmans Publishing Co.

Lawson, R. (1996, June). World Adventism is becoming worldly. *Spectrum, 25,* 4.

Marx, K. (1859). A contribution to the critique of Hegel's philosophy of right. In K. Marx, *Early Writings.*

Marx, K. (1972). Contribution to the critique of Hegel's philosophy of right: Introduction. In R. C. Tucker (Ed.), *The Marx-Engels Reader.* New York: W.W. Norton and Co., Inc.

Moberg, D. O. (1962). *The church as a social institution.* Englewood Cliffs, NJ: Prentice-Hall, Inc.

Moon, J. A. (2003, Spring). The Adventist trinity debate. Part 1: Historical overview. *Andrews University Seminary Studies, 41*(1), 113–129.

Moon, J. A. (2003, Autumn). The Adventist trinity debate. Part 2: The role of Ellen G. White. *Andrews University Seminary Studies, 41*(2) 275–292.

Pearson, M. (1990). *Early Adventist women: In the shadow of the prophetess. Millennial dreams and moral dilemmas.* Cambridge, England: Cambridge University Press.

Rasi, H. M. Education. GC Departmental Report. *GC Bulletin* 5, 2000.

Seventh-day Adventist World Church Statistics. Retrieved August 14, 2006, from http://www.adventist.org/world_church/facts_and_figures/index. html.en

Van Bemmelen, P. M. (1988). Divine accommodation in religion and scripture. *Journal of Adventist Theological Society, 9,* 221–229.

Watts, K. (1995). Moving away from the table: A survey of historical factors affecting women leaders. In P. A. Habada & R. F. Brillhart (Eds.), *The Welcome Table: Setting a place for ordained women.* Langley Park, MD: Team Press.

White, E. G. (1898, March 22). The laborer is worthy of his hire. *Manuscript 43A.*

White, E. G. (1903). *Education.* Mountain View, CA: Pacific Press Publishing Association.

White, E. G. (1948). *Testimonies for the church,* 7:59. Mountain View, CA: Pacific Press Publishing Association.

Yinger, J. M. (1970). *The scientific study of religion.* New York: Macmillan.

CHAPTER FOUR

FAITH/DISCIPLINE INTEGRATION THROUGH SOCIOLOGY

This chapter elaborates on the faith/learning integration construct, surveying the various ways in which the concept has been viewed over time. It embraces and discusses Nelson's (1987) three-pronged model of compatibalist, reconstructionalist, and transformationalist integration as a useful guide to understanding faith/discipline integration. It identifies several relevant scriptural passages deemed foundational to the discussion of various sociology topics. The notions of institution building, the deconstruction of dualities and dichotomies, and ideal/deed integration are presented as sub-types of Nelson's model.

The body of literature on the integration of faith and learning is appreciably growing. Though the documentation of this literature is fairly recent, the application of the faith/learning concept is recognizable in educational practice of a much earlier time. Before the Middle Ages, religion and learning seemed inseparable, with the focus of education being on the impartation of literacy skills to enable students to document, among other things, the principles of their faith (Badley, 1994).

However, this close union between religion and the formal process of learning was somewhat derailed by the Enlightenment, which emphasized the distinction between faith and empirical rationality. Enlightenment thinkers demonstrated a clear preference for empirical rationality and thus for the secularization of the educative process. One consequence of this emphasis was the strong secular orientation that characterized higher education during the eighteenth and nineteenth centuries. Consequently, in the early years of the twentieth century, many universities in the United States of America and Canada opted for totally secular curricula. Marsden (1997) notes that this trend, in which attempts were made to replace religious authority by secular authority, continues to undermine confidence in the education system, particularly for fundamentalists who would rather have a sharp separation between secular learning and religion.

Opinions on the learning/faith connection were tempered somewhat in the post-war years with the advent of the evangelical movement and its more inclusive theological posture, paving the way for the current surge of interest in the integration of faith and learning. Evangelicals, unlike their fundamentalist[1] counterparts, were interested in the interplay between religion and the rest of society. As a result of their efforts, new seminaries and liberal arts colleges came into being (Carpenter & Shipps, 1987). These schools sought to maintain their conservative theological stance, while neither isolating themselves from current academic issues nor having their identity buried in these issues.

During this period, serious attempts were made to articulate the conceptual and operational meaning of the integration of faith and learning. Beginning with Blamires (1950), a number of scholars (Beck, 1991; Gaebelein, 1954; Holmes, 1975; Ryan, 1950; Sikora, 1966; Wilkes, 1991) have sought in various ways to delineate the parameters of the concept. Blamires (1950), for example, though not employing the current integration of faith and learning jargon, recognized the need for the curriculum to be under the influence of all aspects of Christian learning. Later, Gaebelein (1954), who thought of integration as a living union of the various elements of the education process with the pattern of God's truth, expressed similar ideas. Focusing on ways in which teachers relate to the concept, Holmes (1975) identified four teaching models: *complete disjunction*, in which teachers keep the worlds of faith and learning apart; *injunction*, in which teachers point out differences between the two domains; *conjunction*, in which teachers emphasize the natural points of correspondence between the two; and *fusion*, in which teachers present the two domains as one unified reality.

More recently, Badley (1994), seeking to systematize the various strands contributed to the faith/learning integration theme, identified the five variants of fusion, incorporation, correlational, dialogical, and perspectival integration. Fusion integration suggests an additive model, with something new resulting from the interaction. Whereas incorporation integration implies that either of the two elements is subsumed by the other, correlational integration is approach driven and merely indicates that the learning process is under the influence of faith. The process deepens

---

1. While the two terms are often used interchangeably, Evangelicals are distinguished from fundamentalists by the former's less rigid, more liberal position on social issues.

in dialogical integration, where dialogue between the two entities is facilitated and broadens in perspectival integration, which conceives of the entire education process from a faith perspective. Perspectival integration corresponds with what Korniejczuk and Kijai (1994) call deliberate integration, or "...the process of consciously infusing the formal curriculum with the God-centered Christian world view" (p. 80).

Despite the growing literature on the integration of faith and learning, Badley (1994) suggests that this term represents "a slogan in serious need of unpacking" (p. 17). This chapter examines in greater detail the meaning of the integration of faith and learning concept through the lens of the interactionist, delineating three ways in which one may fruitfully put the concept to use.

Interactionism of Faith/Learning Integration

Interactionists highlight the non-deterministic nature of social behavior. They reject the idea of human behavior being a mere stimulus-response exercise and embrace the view that it is contextually constructed (Blumer, 1969; Rose, 1962). Context in the interactionist's view is inclusive and may refer to ideas, objects, relationships, statuses, roles, and other variables that may constitute a social situation. Moreover, interactionists eschew the notion of a passive actor and underscore the interactional, proactive, creative dimension of behavior. Meaning, from this viewpoint, is not given in things and edicts but is rather contingent upon the interactional process. Interactionists, according to Blumer (1969), make the assumptions that (1) humans act based on the meaning they attribute to the things they encounter, (2) humans create meaning in interaction with others, and (3) humans interpret and modify created meanings by situation. While the conceptual thrust of this chapter is guided by the interactionist perspective, the biblical view of the redemptive process provides the benchmark for the analysis.

Conceptual Background

Conceptualized within the framework of the Christian worldview, education responds to the challenge of the human condition. The Apostle Paul describes our condition as sinful, short of the glory of God, and devoid of good works (Rom. 3:25). He paints a picture of broken and fractured relationships, not only in terms of our estrangement from God but also in our adversarial relationships with one another.

The Genesis account (Gen. 3:10) captures this state of alienation in its depictions of Adam and Eve—hiding from God in fear, conscious of their nakedness—and of the first human offspring, Cain, who, having killed Abel, remonstrates with God over his responsibility as his brother's keeper (Gen. 4:9). The first human family thus has been plunged into an existential crisis in which each is isolated from the interactional process through which humans principally experience the essence of being. This isolation has occurred both vertically (from God) and horizontally (from each other). The death knell for the human family thus has been sounded, for outside of the God/human interactional process, the human person perishes. Indeed the Apostle Paul pointed out that in "Him [God] we live and move and have our being" (Acts 17:28). However, it is within the flow of the human/human interactional context that this God/human interaction becomes meaningful, plausible, and demonstrable.

This was the focus of the incarnation. Christ became incarnated (the God/human reconnect) and dwelt (became a part of the human/human interactional process) among us (John 1:14) in order to reestablish the God/human connection and to set in motion the process of de-alienated human/human interchanges. Christ's mission, that of "reconciling the world unto himself" (2 Cor. 5:14), was one of addressing this two-fold brokenness of the human condition. This divine initiative, aimed at the restoration of the human family to oneness with God and each other, has been committed to us for perpetuity.

While some (Curran, 1972; Sartre, 1957) have humanistically framed the holistic approach to education, including its redemptive dimension, White (1903) succinctly captures the Christian perspective when she observes that the work of education and the work of redemption are one (p. 31). She crystallizes the position by suggesting that education comprehends all the faculties and the entire life span of humans in their preparation for the joys of service in this world and the next. Within this perspective, and against this conceptual overview, this chapter focuses on the integration of faith and learning from the interactionist perspective.

For the purpose of the present discussion, integration of faith and learning will refer to any activity or phenomenon in the teaching/learning situation (including concept/process deconstruction, teaching strategy, curriculum content, or personal influence) that promotes and facilitates the growth of faith in the human/divine interactional process. Faith/learning integration is viewed here as a process outcome; the focus is on the teaching/learning dynamic insofar as it impacts learners' attitudes toward the redemptive process. In this light, integration takes place so long as the teaching/learning situation results in behaviors and attitudes that facilitate the God/human and human/human restorative, reconnection process.

Approaches to Faith/Learning (Discipline) Integration

Against this backdrop, three fundamental strategies with subtypes are presented as useful approaches to faith/discipline integration. Critical to the success of the faith/discipline integration project as it is pursued within the discipline of sociology are the identification and articulation of specific strategies that can facilitate authentic integration. The utility of such an exercise lies in the guidance and direction it can provide practitioners and theorists in their efforts towards integration. Over the models of faith/ learning integration previously discussed, Nelson's (1987) three-pronged, compatibalist, reconstructuralist, and transformationalist model serves as a useful sensitizing guide.

In compatibalist integration, areas of commonality between the Christian worldview and an academic discipline (sociology in our case) are identified and discussed in an informed and appealing manner. For Wolfe (1987), these areas of integration should include at least common assumptions and concerns shared by the two entities. Many such areas exist for sociology and Christianity, but two examples seem obvious: (1) the view that the group is the basic unit of analysis and (2) the position that groups consist of interconnected parts. As previously intimated, both the Bible, the principal guidebook for Christians, and sociology present the group as the basic unit of analysis. This point was presented in Chapter One with the support of relevant Scriptural passages, underscoring the necessity of the group as the basis of human goodness and self-realization.

It is not just the group per se that is highlighted for its value to human life and society. Both sociologists and the authors of the Bible emphasize the importance of the interconnected nature of groups. Sociologists, particularly those of the functionalist variety, see social groups and society itself as an integrated unit. Therefore, when subunits (social institutions) do not support and complement each other, the unit (society) malfunctions and social problems arise. In a similar way, Paul likens the church of God to the human body, consisting of many members working for the benefit of each other and the entire unit. "Whether one member suffer, all the members suffer with it; or one member be honoured, all the members rejoice with it" (1 Cor. 12:26).

These are but two areas of compatibility between sociology and the Christian faith. Many other such commonalities await identification and articulation. A teacher of sociology can do this in his or her own teaching by beginning each lecture with a Scriptural passage that ties in with the particular sociological concept to be discussed in that lecture. Table 4.1 cross-references the topics typically covered in an introductory sociology text and the main ideas discussed under such topics with matching biblical passages.

Table 4.1
Integrating Biblical Concepts in the Teaching of Sociology Principles

Course Topics	Main Ideas	Biblical Reference
The Sociological Perspective	(a) Human behavior is group based. (b) Our ideas and behaviors are framed by social facts.	Genesis 1:27 suggests that humans need others. Matthew 28:19 suggests that the divine is grounded in groups.
Culture and Social Structure	Culture is created and is the chief medium of our social, religious, ideational, and perhaps spiritual development.	Psalm 87:6 indicates that God takes into account the circumstances of our life in judging us. Romans 12:1 suggests that Christians are shaped by their cosmos. Genesis 2:19 suggests that God invites humans to participate in naming (creating meaning for) the world.

Course Topics	Main Ideas	Biblical Reference
Socialization	Human beings are not born with skills, dispositions, values, and ideas; these are acquired through groups in society.	Luke 1:52 tells us that Jesus developed (socialized) holistically. Deuteronomy 6:6-8 suggests that God's commands are learned interactively (through the process of discussion and teaching).
Social Research	Knowledge is socially created. It is the basis of the meaning order of society.	Genesis 2:19 states that Adam was asked to generate names for the animals. This co-creative role is carried on in social research. 2 Corinthians 10:5 challenges the Christian to produce an alternative to imagination and knowledge that opposes God.
Bureaucracy, Formal Organization	Formal organizations characterize all human relationships. Through these the needed administrative and leadership functions are met.	Romans 12:8 and 1 Corinthians 12:28 suggest that God has gifted individuals in the church with administrative and leadership skills.
Deviance and Social control	Deviance is socially defined and produced and is contingent upon time, place, occasion, and status.	James 4:1 suggests that the source of deviance is within us.

Course Topics	Main Ideas	Biblical Reference
Stratification	Resources are unequally allocated to people in society on the basis of chosen factors. It must be distinguished from differentiation, which relates to difference in function.	Acts 10:34 suggests that God treats us all equally. Matthew 5:45 suggests that God's general goodwill is equally exercised toward the just and unjust.
Race and Ethnicity	The unequal allocation of resources is justified on the basis of race and ethnicity.	Acts 17:26 tells us that God has made all humans of the same blood. Romans 3:28 suggests there is no division by race or gender for those who are in Christ.
The Family	Family is the most important agency (unit) for primary socialization.	Genesis 2:27 suggests that God mandated marriage as a necessary social institution.
Politics/Economy	Humans need the economic institution for the creation and distribution of goods and services and the political institution for the regulation and orderly operation of social life.	Exodus 20:9 suggests that work as an institution was ordained by God. Daniel 4:32 suggests that God sets up political institutions and takes them down.
Education	Education is the chief agency for the social reproduction of society.	Proverbs 7:11 instructs us to "train up a child...."
Religion	Religion provides the chief source of meaning to the lives of people and is largely social.	James 1:27 and Micah 6:8 suggest that religion is vested human interaction.

Reconstructionist Integration

Reconstructionists dispute the claim that academic disciplines are autonomous. They view the idea that academic disciplines are distinct from and independent of each other as counter-integrative. Specifically, reconstructionists argue that the idea of autonomous discipline stands opposed to the process of "...bringing into captivity every thought to the obedience of Christ" (2 Cor. 10:5). Reconstructionists accordingly respond to this dilemma by suggesting "that it should be rejected outright and remade from the ground up from a biblical foundation" (Harris, 2004, p. 226). Here integration is roundabout. The idea is to demonstrate through empirical research and reasoned deduction that flaws exist in the epistemological assumption of empirical science. Unlike the compatibalist model, the goal in this venture is to show that the assumptions/concerns of Scripture and those of the particular discipline in question are not compatible. It is rather a kind of rethinking and reworking of the discipline to make it "submissive" to Scripture, if only by demonstrating the superior insight of Scripture over that of the particular discipline. This ideal may be pursued in at least two different ways: either (1) by critiquing current theories and scientific findings, using the biblical perspective as the guide, or (2) through the deconstruction of dualities and dichotomies, which are explained below.

In the first instance, theories and ideas that flaunt the authority of Scripture are put to the test through rigorous evaluation. Consider, for example, the positivist claim that non-empirical reality is but a figment of the imagination. Such a claim can be countered by the observation that empiricists have no authoritative, foolproof way beyond the broad assumptions they make about reality to support this claim. Furthermore, it can be pointed out that the very belief of empirical science in the inevitability of progress parallels the biblical view that things seen are preceded by things not seen.

A belief in progress, the view that we can improve upon and transcend current realities, is not always based on empirical proofs; it is at best an assumed possibility. Yet it is this positive disposition toward the unknown that fuels research efforts. So we search for cures for AIDS, cancer, and Parkinson's disease and relate to the search as if the outcome sought is sure. Certainly, this is a valuable attitude without which little progress will be made. But it is faith-based. Now, if we peeled back the scientific view of progress, we should find somewhere in that deconstructed piece the unstated assumption that the seen and known emerge from the unseen and unknown. The empiricist's claim regarding the inevitability of progress may be more faith-based than the empiricist is prepared to admit. In this way, disciplines that at first appeared to be either superior to or disjunctive with Scripture can be shown to be conformable to the faith principle of Scripture that sustains the Christian perspective.

Certainly, one can find other creative ways of subjecting the claims of secular scholarship to the crucible of biblical insights. Double blind studies on prayer seem to be a step in this direction. In these studies, researchers identified persons who stood in need of healing or other forms of help and prayed for them without their knowledge. The results revealed that the "prayed for" had their needs met more significantly than those not prayed for (Cantrell, 2000; McCarthy, 2002). The evidence suggests that prayer makes a difference in the lives of people for whom it is offered. Further, this demonstration is also an indication that the effects of prayer go beyond the placebo effect. It amounts to more than the effect of an artifact of the mind on the body.

Deconstruction of Dichotomies

Another way in which the reconstructionist's strategy at faith/learning integration may be pursued is through the deconstruction of dualities and dichotomies. Indeed, the challenge of the human condition is evident not only in the estrangement of humans from God and each other, as alluded to earlier, but also in the constructs and categories that people generate and employ as tools in their attempt to make sense of the world about them. The reality of people's spiritual and social alienation is conveyed through words. Through words these forms of alienation are subtly perpetuated. Words are not phenomena neutral; they illuminate the meaning of some phenomena, while masking the properties of others. This is especially true of certain categories and dichotomies, several of which have been proposed in sociology: the individual and society, agency and social structure, and the micro and macro, just to name a few.

Despite attempts to de-emphasize the socially-imposed lines of de-marcation between these constructs and efforts aimed at pointing out their dialectical nature, notions of their distinctiveness persist. The truth is that once meanings are given to dichotomous constructs, and boundaries are imposed around them, the process of social sedimentation sets in to ensure their permanence. In other words, once meanings have been constructed and are in use, attitudes tend to harden around them. Thus, constructed categories come to be treated as if they existed on their own and are independent of human effort.

Such rigid views of dichotomous categories ignore their socially-constructed nature and impose upon them a false permanence. Indeed, to treat ideas as if they were self-perpetuating and as if they existed outside the confines of time and circumstance is to attribute to them divine qualities. In this sense Christian teachers and students must be able to deal with dichotomies and categories in a constructive way, placing them within the context of social interaction. Dealing with dichotomous constructs in this way recognizes the interplay between the particular circumstances of individuals' lives and the wider social context in which these individuals live (Mills, 1959). Thus, this sociological imagination helps us appreciate how the ways in which people act and the things they make, preserve, destroy, or remake—whether concrete or abstract—are all influenced by their personal backgrounds and the larger socio-cultural milieu in which they transact.

The capacity to see one's behavior as a function of one's personal background and the broader social context is relevant to the reconciliatory role to which teachers have been called. A major feature of that role has to do with disabusing the mind of misconceptions and ideas that distort the human/divine relationship. An accurate portrayal of that relationship presents humans as co-creators in the social sense. But this relationship is denied in the subject/object dichotomy, effectively blurring a true understanding of the reconciliation process in which God seeks to return humans to their original relationship with Him.

Let us examine this subject/object dichotomous construct and point out both where it limits our understanding of phenomena and impedes the interaction process. The subject/object dichotomy presents two visions of reality, with the inherent presupposition that these visions are mutually exclusive. Those of the objectivist persuasion, positivists, recognize a reality that is independent of our doing. On the other hand, those of the subjectivist orientation, constructionists, contend that reality is not independent of the subject. Positivists, therefore, advocate a method of knowing that is detached and impersonal, arguing that since what is to be known lies outside the inquiring mind, deliberate efforts must be exercised to keep the subjectivity (feelings, emotions, and cognitions) of the inquirer from contaminating the knowing process. The constructionists have rejected this formula of knowing, pointing out that what becomes known cannot be independent of the characteristics of the knowing mind and is therefore an outcome of the mind. What is of interest is the view that knowledge that emerges from the application of the positivist approach should be given priority over knowledge that derives from the interpretivist's (subjectivist's) approach.

The logic that informs this dichotomous treatment of the process of knowing is flawed. For example, the separateness imposed by the positivist upon the relationship between the known and the knower denies any creative interaction between the two. The knower simply takes in the known, the already-created meaning order with its ready-made categories—constructs and all.

However, this knower-known dichotomy is falsified by the invitation God extended to Adam to share in the creation process. The author of Genesis records that Adam was asked to name the animals (Gen. 2:19, 20) and dress and keep the garden (Adam's world—Gen. 2:15). This "naming" and "dressing" of the world are eminently creative activities (Friere, 1985) and constitute the basis of the world's meaning order. Thus, one's restoration in the image of God implies not only a restoration of original capacities but also a recognition and facilitation of the divinely assigned, co-creative role of humans in the restorative process as well. As pointed out before, the subject/object (knower/known) divide advanced by the positivist disallows an appreciation of this process and certainly denies its reality.

Positivists, therefore, tend to present a reality that implies the non-participation of humans in its construction; constructionists, by contrast, blunder in the opposite extreme in positing a reality that is the mere construction of humans. From the viewpoint of the latter, God and other extraterrestrial life forms, such as angels, are but social creations—figments of the imagination—and therefore have no existence independent of the subjective construction of social actors. Thus, while the objectivist view denies humans' co-participation in the creative/re-creative process of the world, the constructionist vision leaves humans without the empowering and transforming power of an objective God whose existence remains separate and independent of human doings. However, from the interactionist standpoint, the truth about the subject/object relationship lies neither in the claim of the objectivist nor the counterclaim of the subjectivist; the truth lies in the creative synthesis resulting from subject and object interaction.

While interactionists recognize that social structure and social objects pre-date current social actors, they nonetheless argue for the interdependence of the two. Though the goals and interactions of social actors are informed by the external social structure, the social structure itself is dependent upon the interaction of social actors. An ongoing object/subject (social structure/social actors) interaction makes for the mutual sustenance and perpetuation of the interacting elements. Thus, the objective social order is reinforced, maintained, and transformed by social actors as much as social actors are facilitated by this order. In a similar way, and as begun in the Garden of Eden with Adam, God (the objective divine Other) invites humans and engages them endlessly in the material (dressing) and non-material (naming) restoration of the world and themselves. In this encounter, humans experience continual renewal and sustenance, while the God image in them is consciously forged and revealed to the world.

Teachers facilitate clarity in the understanding of and faith in the restorative process when they utilize student-centered teaching/learning techniques, especially collaborative efforts, and when they identify and deconstruct dichotomies (i.e., point out the social nature of their constituents) that deny and obscure understanding of the God/human interactional process. In other words, teachers need to take time to underscore the point that while many of our ideas are socially created, this does not deny the human/divine encounter. Indeed, God is fulfilling Himself in humans through His communicated meanings and the flow of ideas that result from human's obedience to Him. When teachers instruct in this way, they facilitate learning outcomes that nourish faith in the ongoing restorative process, reconnecting humankind to God and to one another.

Transformational Integration

Whereas the compatibalist strategy for faith/discipline integration seeks to identify and articulate areas of convergence between faith and learning, both the reconstructionist and transformationalist approaches share a common purpose in their attempts at demonstrating the superior insight of faith claims over those of particular disciplines. Transformationalists have distinguished themselves from reconstructionists in their further emphasis upon "the total transformation of the discipline into its rightful place among the treasures of God's kingdom" (Nelson, 1987, p. 339). In other words, the discipline is accommodated within the bigger picture of faith and thus made to serve faith's end.

More particularly, transformationalists think of genuine integration as involving the heart in its response to the values of love and faith, thus identifying the integration process at the operational level. At this level two variants are recognizable: "institution building" and the blending of ideals and deeds.

Institution Building

One of the more obvious connotations of the transformationalist version of faith/learning integration relates to the subsumption of the contents and methodology of the curriculum under the Christian worldview. According to this perspective, teachers integrate faith and learning when they include biblical ideas about the world and phenomena therein in the teaching of various curriculum areas. One version of this variant of the integration of faith and learning requires that the doctrinal beliefs and practices of particular religious institutions be taught as the legitimate, practical, and true way to know God and to receive salvation. This process results in and has as its ultimate objective the facilitating of faith commitments to a particular worldview. This process can be called "institution building."

While some may disagree with this approach to faith-learning integration for its confinement of faith to a particular denominational perspective, its usefulness in a pluralistic, postmodern world cannot be overemphasized. It provides perspective and a much-needed sorting and unifying mechanism in face of a medley of competing views. Accordingly, Garber (1996) has observed that it is those students who have embraced a worldview who are most able to address the challenge of coherence and truth in a pluralistic society. However, it is not mere preference of one perspective over others that is critical here; rather, it is how that perspective is "passed on" or how students are guided and facilitated in their adoption of that perspective.

While one should not underestimate the content that is communicated in the classroom, one should also note how tremendously important the method of transmission is to recipients—both in their receptivity of the content and in its subsequent effect on them. Communicated ideas by themselves can be cold and meaningless. The context of their communication is what makes the difference. How the heart responds to the values of faith and life is largely a function of the interactional medium through which such values become known. The end state of values depends upon the means of their communication. Accordingly, if teachers are to succeed in passing on the Christian worldview and its associated values through institution building, then the strategies employed for their transmission must take a cue from this principle.

Toward this end, respect for the individual as a free moral agent is paramount and requires the adoption of teaching strategies that facilitate the free-will capacity of the student. Furthermore, such teaching strategies would remove the possibility of the student becoming a "mere reflector of other men's thoughts" (White, 1903, p. 12). Thus a student-centered approach to teaching would help steer the teaching/learning act away from a brainwashing culture in which the one-sided, banking concept of education is utilized (Apple, 1993; Freire, 1985). Brainwashing education not only encourages the unreflective and indiscriminate imbibing of ideas by the student, but by its very nature flies in the face of the God/human restorative process by its failure to engage the student in reflective thinking and learning.

In this connection, Palmer's (1993) characterization of teaching as the creation "of a space in which obedience to truth is practiced" seems particularly appropriate (p. 69). Obedience to truth cannot be coerced or dictated; it must be negotiated and agreed upon within an open interactional milieu. While truth is objective and is ultimately embodied in Jesus, its author and personification, the meaning of truth tends to vary across individual perspectives. Far from being a compromise of truth, this position points instead to the capacity of truth to accommodate several unique patterns of perception and interaction. God meets humans where they are and invites them to the interactional process for the collaborative out-working of His will for them. Thus, Palmer's learning space, which is characterized by openness, boundaries, and hospitality, is close to the ideal milieu for such a negotiation.

The teaching/learning situation in which this strategy is utilized displays openness in the care exercised in examining and removing personal and situational barriers to learning. Related efforts in this vein target areas such as students' motivation, teachers' perception and expectations of student performance, and institutional policies. When learning is open, students and teachers experience a sense of freedom and are motivated to continue in the teaching/learning relationship. Boundaries, on the other hand, ensure that the sense of freedom to act and think does not descend to realms of confusion and chaos. Finally, Palmer (1993) posits that the hospitality dimension of the created learning space makes for classrooms "where every stranger and every strange utterance is met with welcome" (p. 24) and where the necessarily painful aspects of teaching, such as the exposing of ignorance and the challenging of false or partial information, among others, are borne with pleasure. Though difficult, these outcomes can be realized when teachers relinquish the God-like role of superiority and control and are willing to die to self (Smith, 1997). A teaching/learning environment of this sort, whatever the content or values communicated, truly hallmarks the kind of interactional milieu that elicits the heart's response.

Institution building through worldview transmission and the facilitating of faith commitments, when attempted in this vein, is not only defensible but commendable as well. In such a learning space, the following features are easily recognizable:

1. Teachers are as teachable as they expect their students to be.
2. Mutual respect exists between teachers and students.
3. Teachers are sensitive to individual peculiarities, including learning styles, and adopt appropriate measures to meet each need.
4. Teachers demonstrate a loving, caring, non-judgmental attitude toward students. The emphasis is on collaboration rather than competitive, individual efforts.
5. Teachers create an environment that is sufficiently flexible to allow for unfettered inquiry and creativity, yet has enough structure to engender a sense of safety and direction.
6. Teachers are patient, thoughtful, forbearing, and accepting of each other. (This is of special significance since it sets the pace for such interactions between students.)
7. Students are cooperative, respectful, caring, and forgiving.
8. A genuine attempt is made to allow love and caring to pervade the entire classroom atmosphere.

Integration of Ideals and Deeds

The ultimate measure by which success in the process of faith/discipline integration may be judged transcends the conceptual and teaching methods that may have been generated to facilitate that process. It hinges more centrally upon the degree to which those who teach the particular discipline can demonstrate that the principles of their faith inform their daily practice. For this reason, the transfer gap that exists between theory and action constitutes one of the most serious indictments of the Christian worldview. This is a gap between the prescriptive norms and values and the real norms and values that Christians embrace. Indeed, confidence in the efficacy of the restorative plan put in motion for humanity's reconnection to God and to each other stands critically challenged in the face of such a divide. Indeed, much of the institution building we may effect, and the conceptual gaps we may fill, will presently come to naught without the confirming evidence of genuine praxis.

The quintessential role of Christian sociology teachers involves demonstrating evidence and identifying ways of action that underscore the possibility of bridging the divide between the ideals of the Christian faith and the lived experience of Christians. Nurtured by this demonstration, students' commitment grows, their disbelief evaporates, and their faith is confirmed. Younger Christians suffocate in the absence of such teaching; more mature Christians take solace in cold rationality in the face of its absence. Sociology teachers can fruitfully approach this ideal of the demonstration of authentic praxis in at least two ways.

First, students should be organized and encouraged to apply the theories and sociological principles they have learned to solve or alleviate community problems. Too often learning takes place in a theory-tight atmosphere. Not only is the teaching of abstract principles attempted in an abstract manner without concrete examples, but also the relevance of these principles to real-life situations is often veiled by the absence of appropriate projects that address the needs of the surrounding community. Accordingly, work-study projects that target the needs of the school community are certainly in place. The sociology class may be organized around service-related projects that target felt needs in the community, such as helping the community find ways to reduce crime, improve its parks, or bring cheer to senior and special-needs citizens.

Second, students can learn of the possibility of living faith-consistent lives and of finding fulfillment therein. This will occur not only from their own experience of applied theory, as just discussed, but also from the lives of role models. The eagerness with which people listen to others as they tell their stories of faith in action attests to the value of this vicarious means of faith/learning integration. It is truly a prime means for demonstrating the efficacy of the redemptive process.

Accordingly, sociology teachers who have successfully integrated their faith with their discipline in serving their community can be called upon to relate their story to the class. Additionally, those sociologists who have investigated the impact of religion on various aspects of life can be invited to talk about their research. These "models" can be the source of meaning and encouragement to those students who are looking for real life examples upon which to pin their faith. Among the factors that Garber (1996) observed in students who were able to match their ideals and their lived experience were (1) their interaction with teachers whose lives incarnated their world view (that is, teachers who practiced what they preached), and (2) the students forging links with others who shared their worldview (p. 111). The motivation to live a coherent life of faith should not derive exclusively from the lived experience of others, but the social nature of human behavior nonetheless emerges as a potent factor in this context. Students are more likely to believe what they do with others or observe others doing rather than what they are merely told.

Thus when teachers impart values and ideals that are absent in the repertoire of their own conduct, they contribute to the cynicism spawned by what Berger, Berger, and Kellner (1974) captured in their book *The Homeless Mind*. Often, though, it is not the individual lives of teachers that prove disappointing to students who search for real-life examples upon which to base their faith; rather, it is the corporate life of the institution.

Institutions that come under this fault-line are likely to be those that have succumbed to the bureaucratic spirit, where the rational pursuit of set goals is valued more highly than human relationships. One explanation for this outcome may be attributed to the tendency in humans to treat social practices and ideas as if they have a life of their own, independent of people's interaction. Such a tendency not only ignores the social basis of those ideas and practices but also the purpose for which they were meant.

Thus, stakeholders of social institutions frequently tend to lose sight of the social basis of ideas and behave as if people were meant for the good of social ideas and practices, rather the other way around. Leaders tend to forget that institutional polices were made for people and not people for institutional policies. Merton (1938) suggested that when leaders make the process more important than the outcome, both organizations and individuals tend to lose sight of the institution's goal. The result is bureaucratic ritualism characterized by cold formality and a disconnection between people.

Recognition of this tendency, especially by those who manage the day-to-day life of institutions, may prove helpful in identifying and eliminating factors that increase the inconsistency between ideals and practice at the institutional level. Given the powerful impact that institutions tend to have on those who come under their operation, this is especially important. Because of this effect, people generally take their cue for action from institutional patterns and tend—sometimes unconsciously, sometimes consciously—to reproduce those patterns, even when they are not consistent with the world-view of the institution. When this happens, students come to lose faith not only in the institution per se, but also in the vision for which the institution stands. On the other hand, when the lives of Christian teachers and the dominant patterns of Christian institutions in which those students transact are consistent with the ideals and values communicated to them, faith flourishes and doubt in the possibility of a coherent life of faith disappears. Needless to say, such an outcome generates faith in the restorative process.

References

Apple, M. W. (1993). *Official knowledge.* New York: Routledge.

Badley, K. (1994, Spring). The faith/learning integration movement in Christian higher education: Slogan or substance? *Journal of Research on Christian Education, 3*(1), 13–33.

Beck, W. D. (Ed.). (1991). *Opening the American mind.* Grand Rapids, MI: Baker.

Berger, P., Berger, B., & Kellner, H. (1974). *The homeless mind: Modernization and consciousness.* New York: Random.

Blamires, H. (1950). *Repairs the ruins.* London: Geoffrey Bles.

Blumer, H. (1969). *Symbolic interactionism.* Englewood Cliffs, NJ: Prentice-Hall.

Cantrell, R. (2000, August). Evidence of the effect of prayer in medicine. Paper presented at the Conference on Healing [*Christian Medical Foundation International*], Kanuga Conference Center, North Carolina, August 15, 2000.

Carpenter, J. A., & Shipps, K. W. (Eds.). (1987). *Making higher education Christian: The history, purpose, and agenda of evangelical colleges in America.* Grand Rapids, MI: Wm. B. Eerdmans Publishing Co.

Curran, C. A. (1972). *Counseling-learning. A whole-person model for education.* New York: Grune & Stratton.

Freire, P. (1985). *Teachers as cultural workers.* Boulder, CO: Westview.

Gaebelin, F. E. (1954). *The pattern of God's truth: Problems of integration in Christian education.* New York: Oxford University Press.

Garber, S. (1996). *The fabric of faithfulness.* Downers Grove, IL: Inter-Varsity Press.

Harris, R. A. (2004). *The integration of faith and learning: A world view approach.* Eugene, OR: Cascade Books.

Holmes, A. F. (1975). *The idea of a Christian college.* Grand Rapids, MI: Eerdmans.

Korniejczuk, R. I., & Kijai, J. (1994). Integrating faith and learning: Development of a stage model by teacher implementation. *Journal of Research on Christian Education, 3*(1).

Marsden, G. M. (1997). *The outrageous idea of Christian scholarship.* New York: Oxford University Press.

McCarthy, L. F. (2002, February). Prayer's power over your heart. *Vegetarian Times, 294,* 6.

Merton, R. K. (1938). *Sociological ambivalence and other essays.* New York: Free Press.

Mills, C. W. (1959). *The sociological imagination.* London: Oxford University Press.

Nelson, R. R. (1987). Faith-discipline integration: Compatibilist, reconstructionalist, and transformationalist strategies. In H. Heie & D. L. Wolfe (Eds.), *The reality of Christian learning* (pp. 317–39). Grand Rapids, MI: Wm. B. Eerdmans Publishing Co.

Palmer, P. J. (1993). *To know as we are known: Education as a spiritual journey.* San Francisco: Harper.

Rose, A. M. (Ed). (1962). *Human behavior and social processes: An interactionist approach.* London: Routledge & Kegan Paul.

Ryan, J. J. (1950). On the meaning of integration. In R. J. Deferrari (Ed.), *Integration in Catholic colleges and universities* (pp. 10–25). Washington, DC: Catholic University of America Press.

Sartre, J. P. (1957). *Existentialism and human emotions.* New York: Philosophical Library.

Sikora, J. J. (1966). *The Christian intellect and the mystery of being: Reflections of a Maritain Thomist.* The Hague: Martinus Nijoff.

Smith, D. (1997). Christian thinking in education reconsidered. *Spectrum, 27*(1), 9–24.

White, E. G. (1903). *Education.* Mountain View, CA: Pacific Press Publishing Association.

Wilkes, P. (Ed.). (1991). *Christianity challenges the university.* Downers Grove, IL: InterVarsity Press.

Wolfe, D. L. (1987). The line of demarcation between integration and pseudointegration. In H. Heie & D. Wolfe (Eds.), *The Reality of Christian Learning* (pp. 3–11). Grand Rapids, MI: Wm. B. Eerdmans Publishing Co.

CHAPTER FIVE

INTEGRATING SOCIOLOGY WITH THE SEVENTH-DAY ADVENTIST WORLDVIEW

In this chapter, the value of a worldview is discussed. It is suggested that it is basic to the way we make sense of the world. The twenty-eight fundamental beliefs of Seventh-day Adventists are identified as the major reality-framing worldview of this group. It is argued that the study of sociology can be a means through which understanding of elements of the twenty-eight fundamental beliefs can be facilitated and extended.

Careful consideration reveals that all realities, whether natural or social, remain random and chaotic without some appropriate sorting system of meaning. In this light, accepted patterns of order and meaning are necessarily based upon particular ways of seeing and interpreting the world.

While this position presupposes that people make sense of the world in different ways, it does not suggest that each of these ways of making sense of the world is equally valid. What is emphasized in this discussion, however, is the view that order in the human context is perspective-driven. This is not to propose that order (reality) does not exist independent of the particular ways individuals and groups make sense of things. Rather, the suggestion is that these particular ways of making sense of things enable people to access and process objective reality and create their order. Hence, the position that order is perspective-driven is not a denial of the fact that there is an objective reality that is independent of the perceiving mind of humans.

Indeed, insofar as the notion of an "out there" reality advanced by the positivist can be applied to the belief in an extra-human, ultimate divine reality, it is to be devoutly embraced by Christians. But even the divine reality, if it is not "framed" (accommodated within a worldview scheme), remains insubstantial and incomprehensible to the human mind. This position is basic to the sociological perspective, and particularly to the sociology of knowledge tradition, which posits that meanings are attributed to reality within framed contexts (Berger & Luckman, 1966; Clark & Gaede, 1987; Thomas & Znaniecki, 1918).

Faith Perspectives and the Framing of Reality

The meaning-facilitating value of perspectives underscores the relevance and importance of faith-based organizations as reality-framing and sustaining mechanisms. Religion functions not only as a source of meaning and purpose but also as a source of social stability and anchorage as well (Roberts, 2000). For many, religion is the ultimate plausibility structure,[1] the means through which their mind-pictures of life and the world are obtained and maintained. Central to religious organizations as plausibility structures are beliefs and rituals by which those who share a particular worldview are affirmed and energized in their commitment. Just as important and fundamental as these beliefs and rituals are to the life of faith communities, they will not long endure if they are not continually recharged and effectively passed on through time. Kelley (1977) accordingly reminds us that a culture that does not pass on its shared meanings through time will not survive.

Seventh-day Adventism as a faith-based perspective is informed by twenty-eight fundamental, Bible-based doctrinal beliefs that constitute the basic guideposts of conduct and the source of hope for millions of Seventh-day Adventists. These fundamental beliefs "edify the church, preserve the truth, and communicate the gospel in all its richness" (*Seventh-day Adventists Believe...*, 1988, p. viii). The broad membership, and more particularly the stakeholders, share a vested interest in ensuring the preservation and perpetuation of these core beliefs through, among other things, the integration of faith and learning.

This explains why the Seventh-day Adventist church operates more than 6,000 schools from elementary to university levels around the world. These schools pass on the vision and principles of the church as students are socialized into "a useful and joy-filled life fostering friendship with God" (*JRCE*, 2001, p. 349).

---

1. Plausibility structures refer to the social processes and interactions that exist within a network of persons sharing a meaning system. These processes and interactions (e.g., support systems, worship fellowships, etc.) support the meaning system and makes it believable.

Since 1988, the Institute for Christian Teaching, under the aegis of the General Conference of Seventh-day Adventists, encouraged Adventist teachers to explore strategies for integrating faith and discipline. The main vehicles for this undertaking are annual Integration of Faith and Learning Conferences and Christ in the Classroom Conference proceedings. These efforts presume that every subject taught in Adventist schools can and ought to be a vehicle for the preservation and promulgation of the Seventh-day Adventist worldview perspective.

Previous attempts (Dulan, 1999; Matthews, 1999; McBride, 1996) have demonstrated how, within the broad sweep of the faith/learning integration principles, sociology can be such a vehicle. However, no work exists on how specific doctrinal points of the Seventh-day Adventist worldview perspective may be accommodated and conveyed through the teaching and study of the major sociological concepts. The present chapter pursues this task, informed by the position that "the integration of faith and learning is fundamentally an intellectual activity that brings together basic Christian theological understanding and the discipline we teach" (Land, 2000, p. 85).

Obviously, no one-to-one match between the core beliefs of Seventh-day Adventists and the major sociological concepts exists, but reasonable "goodness of fit" can be demonstrated in selected instances. In this regard, sociological concepts can be shown to facilitate Seventh-day Adventists' theological understanding. Hence, in the section that follows, eight of the twenty-eight fundamental beliefs of Seventh-day Adventists have been selected for review. Suggestions are made for how specific sociological concepts can be used as a means by which insights into these beliefs may be gained and communicated.

The Nature of the Fundamental Reality

The second of the twenty-eight fundamental beliefs addresses the question of the nature of the deity. The belief states the following:

> There is one God: Father, Son, and Holy Spirit, a unity of three co-eternal Persons. God is immortal, all-powerful, all-knowing, above all, and ever present. He is infinite and beyond human comprehension, yet known through His self-revelation. He is forever worthy of worship, adoration, and service by the whole creation. (*Seventh-day Adventist Yearbook*, 2005, p. 5)

This belief speaks to the group nature of the deity. It suggests that the identity of the ultimate and transcendent God is vested in "groupness." Though three separate, distinct beings are acknowledged, Seventh-day Adventist Christians, like most other Christians, adopt the biblical, singular view of the Trinity. As was discussed in Chapter One, this approach to the ultimate reality (God) harmonizes with the sociological view that the group constitutes the fundamental reality. Adventist teachers and students of sociology can gain much mileage from this connection in their attempt to use their discipline as a medium to flesh out the meaning of this fundamental doctrinal belief of their church. They may venture to point out that the basic social reality (the group) embraced by sociology corresponds with the ultimate spiritual reality, and that at least on this count sociology reinforces the Seventh-day Adventist Trinitarian position on the deity.

What It Means to Be Human

Seventh-day Adventists believe that humans bear the image of God in their being; they possess free will and the ability to be creative. This position is summarized in the seventh fundamental belief:

> Man and woman were made in the image of God with individuality, the power and freedom to think and to do. Though created free beings, each is an indivisible unity of body, mind, and spirit, dependent upon God for life and breath and all else. When our first parents disobeyed God, they denied their dependence upon Him and fell from their high position under God. The image of God in them was marred and they became subject to death. Their descendants share this fallen nature and its consequences. They are born with weaknesses and tendencies to evil. But God in Christ reconciled the world to Himself and by His Spirit restores in penitent mortals the image of their Maker. Created for the glory of God, they are called to love Him and one another, and to care for their environment. (*Seventh-day Adventist Yearbook*, 2005, p. 5)

Not only does this statement acknowledge the free-will capacity of humans, it also points out their "lostness" and recognizes the possibility for their redemption in Christ. This belief speaks of humankind's possibility of having a relationship with God. Human freedom is, therefore, not uncircumscribed; how humans exercise their free will holds critical implication for their well being. When they exercise free will in defiance of the will of God, they are fated to the baleful consequences of sin (Rom. 6:23). But the weight of humans' fallen nature and the active presence of evil in the world ever operate to incline humans to defy God, outside of the reconciling power of Christ.

Adventist teachers and students of sociology may fit the discussion of this doctrinal belief in their explanation of the sociological position on human nature. As previously indicated (see Chapter Two), the reigning sociological paradigms imply two basic positions on human nature. The conflict and structural functionalist paradigms link human conduct in a direct way to the impact of the social milieu. The environment is deemed to be determinant, and human beings rise or fall with the immediate and broader circumstances of their lives. In these accounts the "creatureliness" of humans is accentuated, and we see more of the human being that has lost the image of God, a being almost totally dependent upon environment for survival and meaning. The suggestion is that, in the absence of societal norms and practices, human beings drift into a state of disorder captured by Thomas Hobbes (1909) as the conflict of "every man against every man" (p. 96). In this light, it is the "social contract," operating through societal norms, that rescues humans from their lostness. The social structure thus becomes the redemptive mechanism, without which humans simply stagnate in a state of "normlessness," forfeit the condition for peaceful coexistence, and become enveloped in the "war of all against all" (Velasquez, 2002, p. 255).

This emphasis on the social structure as a liberating mechanism parallels the biblical view that the human person is naturally evil and needs an extra-individual source of power for survival and salvation. While sociology qua sociology confines the source of that power to the social world, Seventh-day Adventism underscores the divine spiritual reality as the ultimate source. Thus the two positions by their common emphasis on the external source of the power required for humanity's rescue are joined.

Sociologists of the symbolic interactionist persuasion present a somewhat different picture, one that better harmonizes with the Adventist view of human nature. Recognizing the free will and creative capacity of humans, symbolic interactionists acknowledge humanity's ability to construct reality within some finite context.

Whereas the symbolic interactionist conceives of the limits placed on the exercise of free will in terms of the various social situations, the Seventh-day Adventist position discussed here represents these limits chiefly as humans' inborn "weakness and tendencies to evil" (*Seventh-day Adventist Yearbook*, 2005, p. 5). However, in spite of this emphasis that Adventists place on the fundamental role that the sin factor (God-human alienation) plays on humans' expression of free will, Adventists still appreciate the impact of the social situation on such expressions. In spite of their acknowledgment of the built-in weakness of humans, Seventh-day Adventists do not see the sinful human nature as ultimately determinant. Humans can exercise their free will to enter into an interactive relationship with Christ, who then empowers them to heights of nobility and acts of righteousness. This is the basis on which Paul declares, "I can do all things through Christ which strengthens me" (Phil. 4:13). On the same basis, John reminds us that the person who is born of God does not sin (1 John 3:9). Thus, the symbolic interactionist perspective, with its emphasis on human free will, lends itself to a theoretical account of Adventists' position on human nature. More particularly, the symbolic interactionist paradigm positions the Adventist teacher of sociology to fruitfully account for the interplay between human free will, humans' inborn weaknesses and tendencies to sin, and the empowering grace of Christ.

The Dialectics of Life

Seventh-day Adventists view human existence in this world against the larger backdrop of a cosmic conflict. The "great controversy," as the conflict is characterized in Adventist theology, pits the forces of good against the forces of evil in a protracted struggle that began in heaven. This position is detailed in the eighth doctrinal statement:

> All humanity is now involved in the great controversy between Christ and Satan regarding the character of God, His law, and His sovereignty over the universe. This conflict originated in heaven when a created being, endowed with freedom of choice, in self-exaltation became Satan, God's adversary, and led into rebellion a portion of the angels. He introduced the spirit of rebellion into this world when he led Adam and Eve into sin. This human sin resulted in the distortion of the image of God in humanity, the disordering of the created world, and its eventual devastation at the time of the worldwide flood. Observed by the whole creation, this world became the arena of the universal conflict, out of which the God of love will ultimately be vindicated. To assist His people in this controversy, Christ sends the Holy Spirit and the loyal angels to

guide, protect, and sustain them in the way of salvation. (*Seventh-day Adventist Yearbook*, 2005, p. 5)

While this controversy alienates the attention and allegiance of angels and humans from God, it is nonetheless the means through which "the God of love will ultimately be vindicated" (*Seventh-day Adventist Yearbook*, 2005, p. 5). While some will be vanquished (as in the case of the deceived angels), others in the same cosmic tension will be victors, becoming more than conquerors through Christ (Rom. 8:37). In others words, the Great Controversy does not take its toll of victims without yielding its harvest of victors. Like the patriarch Job, many Christians, though sorely tested by the controversy, will maintain their integrity and eventually emerge from the conflict more refined and endowed than they were at the beginning of their experience (1 Pet. 4:12, 13; Job 42:10).

The Great Controversy is waged on the social, mental, physical, religious, and spiritual fronts of our lives. Basic to the controversy is the devil's attempt to build a case against the integrity of God by describing Him to humans as selfish and unloving. God, on the other hand, commits Himself to the human race in a ceaseless demonstration of love and care that peaked at the Cross. This places humans in the tension-filled situation of having to constantly make choices between the proffering of God and the counter-propositions of the devil. How humans choose is often reflected on the various fronts listed above and, more importantly, determines how the controversy is resolved in their own lives.

Seventh-day Adventist teachers and students of sociology may address this doctrinal belief through the conflict and symbolic interactionist paradigms. In both these paradigms, social life and thought are viewed dialectically. The basic point of the dialectical argument is that social life emerges from the tension of opposing forces. Dialectical development results from the contradictions inherent[2] in objects and phenomena. The process is marked by the passage of quantitative into qualitative changes, and the negation of negation, that is, the replacement of the old by the new (Afanasyev, 1965).

Examined in light of the dialectical process, the great controversy can be grasped in terms of the struggle of the opposing forces of good and

---

2. Inherent contradictions, in which opposites co-exist in a single entity and drive its becoming, are a feature of most phenomena and objects. For example, the building up (cell reproduction) and the breaking down (cell destruction) processes of the human body are cases in point.

evil. Through such an examination of the great controversy and through real-life experience of it, teachers and students alike may see improvement in the quality of their ideational, religious, social, and spiritual lives. They may note that just as the old gives way to the new and the outmoded to the relevant in the process of social and mental development, even so the superior force of God's love eventually overcomes the inferior selfishness of the devil as God is vindicated through the unselfish lives of His children.

Holistic and Communitarian Beliefs

Seventh-day Adventists are explicitly holistic and communitarian in their beliefs about humans in general and the church in particular. Fundamental belief number eleven clearly conveys the idea of the communitarian nature of the church:

> The church is the community of believers who confess Jesus Christ as Lord and Saviour. In continuity with the people of God in Old Testament times, we are called out from the world; and we join together for worship, for fellowship, for instruction in the Word, for the celebration of the Lord's Supper, for service to all mankind, and for the worldwide proclamation of the gospel. The church derives its authority from Christ, who is the incarnate Word, and from the Scriptures, which are the written Word. The church is God's family; adopted by Him as children, its members live on the basis of the new covenant. The church is the body of Christ, a community of faith of which Christ Himself is the Head. The church is the bride for whom Christ died that He might sanctify and cleanse her. At His return in triumph, He will present her to Himself a glorious church, the faithful of all the ages, the purchase of His blood, not having spot or wrinkle, but whole and without blemish. (*Seventh-day Adventist Yearbook*, 2005, p. 6)

Here the church is described as a community of believers, with Jesus as its head and source authority, called out for the purpose of joint fellowship, worship, common instruction in the Scriptures, and service to the world. Of all the doctrinal positions of the Seventh-day Adventist church, this one, with its communitarian focus, is perhaps the most sociological. It is not difficult to find parallel concepts and constructs in sociology through which this doctrinal belief can be conveyed in the classroom. Indeed, sociology is largely the study of human community.

Teachers may find it useful in discussing the features of a community to use the Seventh-day Adventist church as an example. They can point out that the features that characterize communities in general also underlie the operation of the church. Specifically, teachers and students can choose to discuss the functions of norms, values, group dynamics, and the role of authority figures as these relate to the stable and changing patterns of the church as a community.

Unity in Church

The focus on the church as a community logically extends into the doctrinal belief regarding the unity of the church as described in the thirteenth fundamental belief:

> The church is one body with many members, called from every nation, kindred, tongue, and people. In Christ we are a new creation; distinctions of race, culture, learning, and nationality, and differences between high and low, rich and poor, male and female, must not be divisive among us. We are all equal in Christ, who by one Spirit has bonded us into one fellowship with Him and with one another; we are to serve and be served without partiality or reservation. Through the revelation of Jesus Christ in the Scriptures we share the same faith and hope, and reach out in one witness to all. This unity has its source in the oneness of the triune God, who has adopted us as His children. (*Seventh-day Adventist Yearbook*, 2005, p. 6)

This doctrinal tenet speaks to the relational ideal to which Seventh-day Adventists aspire. The ideal fits well with what Ferdinand Tonnies (1988) describes as Gemeinschaft, a community in which the welfare of the group is primary, and where personal ties, intimacy, and a sense of togetherness hallmark interpersonal relationships. Where this relational ideal is not reached, it can be pointed out that forces such as the size of the group, industrialization, and urbanization may be among the inhibitory factors. For example, Tonnies blames the industrialization of Western societies for the decline of Gemeinschaft-type relationships and their replacement with Gessellschaft-type relationships, where impersonality, anonymity, and self-interest predominate.

Wholeness in Christ

Not only do Seventh-day Adventists pursue communal concord as an ideal, they seek it in specific ways and with the awareness of certain necessary conditions. Fundamental belief number twenty-one identifies the levels at which communal harmony and the conditions that facilitate it are sought:

> We are called to be a godly people who think, feel, and act in harmony with the principles of heaven. For the Spirit to recreate in us the character of our Lord we involve ourselves only in those things which will produce Christlike purity, health, and joy in our lives. This means that our amusement and entertainment should meet the highest standards of Christian taste and beauty. While recognizing cultural differences, our dress is to be simple, modest, and neat, befitting those whose true beauty does not consist of outward adornment but in the imperishable ornament of a gentle and quiet spirit. It also means because our bodies are the temples of the Holy Spirit, we are to care for them intelligently. Along with adequate exercise and rest, we are to adopt the most healthful diet possible and abstain from the unclean foods identified in the Scriptures. Since alcoholic beverages, tobacco, and the irresponsible use of drugs and narcotics are harmful to our bodies, we are to abstain from them as well. Instead, we are to engage in whatever brings our thoughts and bodies into the discipline of Christ, who desires our wholesomeness, joy, and goodness...
> (*Seventh-day Adventist Yearbook*, 2005, p. 7)

This belief underscores the Adventists' holistic approach to life and suggests that godly living involves their thinking and feeling no less than their behaviors in areas of attire and physical exercise. These aspects of their lives are expected to be integrated in keeping with biblical principles, reflecting the Holy Spirit's recreative work in them. This holistic position, as pointed out in Chapter Three, is logically sociological, since it allows us to be sensitive to and relate to all aspects of life as interconnected pieces.

Teachers and students of sociology may glean deeper insights into this doctrinal tenet in their application of Durkheim's notion of social facts. Here teachers in particular can point out to students that their own patterns of thinking, feeling, and acting to a large extent are informed by other such patterns that either predate them or are independent of them. Students can thus grasp the connection between their own feeling and thinking and those of past and current generations. Thus, it can be seen that we do not individually create the beliefs and values we embrace—they are the legacies of past generations or the regenerative work of the Holy Spirit in the hearts and policy decisions of committee members. The same idea can be grasped when the concept of group dynamics is examined. What should become clear in this encounter is that our thinking, feeling, and behavior patterns are much more group-bound than we often would like to think.

Focus on the Family

The marriage and family institutions occupy a central place not only in the doctrinal posture of the Seventh-day Adventist church but in its educational and evangelistic practices as well. Seventh-day Adventists, for example, believe that the marriage institution is God-ordained. Further, it is their view that when the married couple conduct themselves in a manner consistent with biblical principles, their relationship becomes the very expression of "the relationship between Christ and the Church" (*Seventh-day Adventist Yearbook*, 2005, p. 7). More fully expressed, Adventists believe the following:

Marriage was divinely established in Eden and affirmed by Jesus to be a lifelong union between a man and a woman in loving companionship. For the Christian, a marriage commitment is to God as well as to the spouse, and should be entered into only between partners who share a common faith. Mutual love, honor, respect, and responsibility are the fabric of this relationship, which is to reflect the love, sanctity, closeness, and permanence of the relationship between Christ and His church. Regarding divorce, Jesus taught that the person who divorces a spouse, except for fornication, and marries another, commits adultery. Although some family relationships may fall short of their ideal, marriage partners who fully commit themselves to each other in Christ may achieve loving unity through the guidance of the Spirit and the nurture of the church. God blesses the family and intends that its members shall assist each other toward complete maturity. Parents are to bring up their children to love and obey the Lord. By their example and their words they are to teach them that Christ is a loving disciplinarian, ever tender and caring, who wants them to become members of His body, the family of God. Increasing family closeness is one of the earmarks of the final gospel message. (*Seventh-day Adventist Yearbook*, 2005, p. 7)

Implicit in the twenty-second fundamental belief are principles on divorce, relationship repair, parental discipline, marital fidelity, and family togetherness. The importance of these areas to the well being of the family is well known, as is indicated by the attention given to them in current sociological literature and also in other social science research projects.

The inclusion of this doctrinal belief in the teaching and study of sociology should not prove too difficult, given the available avenues of expression. Most principles of sociology texts include at least one full chapter on the family. In addition, several sociology courses address the family from the sociological perspective, while numerous videos, family resource centers, personnel, and books are available to the teacher and student. Many of these are tailored to the Adventist positional view on the family and may be effectively utilized by the sociology teacher and student. Of special relevance in this connection are the writings of Ellen G. White on the family. Finally, Adventist teachers and students of sociology may wish to do their own research on the family, examining in particular Adventist families, in light of the doctrinal tenets on the family.

The Eschatological Vision of Seventh-day Adventists and Its Sociological Parallel

Much of the buoyancy and optimism that sustains Seventh-day Adventist Christians in the face of the deepening crises of the "great controversy" can be attributed to their eschatological vision of the world. Seventh-day Adventists subscribe to the belief of the second advent of Christ, who at His coming will terminate the reign of sin and set up His kingdom of righteousness, bringing to an end life as we know it. A new world replaces the old, and sorrow and crying are eliminated. The twenty-seventh fundamental belief captures the scene more precisely:

> On the new earth, in which righteousness dwells, God will provide an eternal home for the redeemed and a perfect environment for everlasting life, love, joy, and learning in His presence. For here God Himself will dwell with His people, and suffering and death will have passed away. The great controversy will be ended, and sin will be no more. All things, animate and inanimate, will declare that God is love; and He shall reign forever. Amen... (*Seventh-day Adventist Yearbook*, 2005, p. 28)

This end-of-time vision can be channeled in the discussion of the futuristic musings of some sociologists who, troubled by the chaos and contradictions of their society, offered their own prophetic solution. August Comte (1855), as previously discussed, sought resolution in the evolution of human progress. Society would, he thought, transcend the theological and metaphysical stages of thinking and advance to the positive stage when empirical science would become the norm. Comte believed this stage would bring resolution to the crisis of the modern world by providing a system of ideas that would guide the reorganization of society (Aron, 1968).

Another sociologist who prophesied the end of the social order was Karl Marx. Despite his clear humanistic, atheistic leanings, he came close to the biblical New Earth ideal in his own vision of a transformed world. In fact, Marx's story of human society seems copied and reworked from the biblical explanation of the fall and eventual restoration of humans. Marx saw human society going through five stages that he referred to as social formations: primitive communalism, slavery, feudalism, capitalism, and communism.

The first and last of these stages are characterized by the absence of class conflict, while the others are conflict-ridden. In primitive communalism, the means of production are owned collectively; inequality and inter-group antagonism are absent. Marx's description sounds remarkably like the Garden of Eden before sin. In the last stage, the working class, having endured the contradictions of a class-based social order, take things into their own hands. They rise up and overthrow the ruling capitalist class that oppresses them, ushering in the final society of classlessness and the absence of inter-group animosity. Marx describes life in this ideal communistic world:

> Society regulates the general production and thus makes it possible to do one thing today and another tomorrow, to hunt in the morning, fish in the afternoon, rear cattle in the evening, criticize after dinner, just as I have a mind, without ever becoming a hunter, fisherman, shepherd, or critic. (Marx & Engles, 1960, p. 22)

In other words, humans are now at the stage where they will have life as they call it. Though Comte and Marx's conceptualizations of these end states of society are ultimately materialistic and secular in connotation, the sociology teacher and student may yet appropriate them to a discussion of the Adventist vision of heaven. Note can be taken of the missing links in the arguments, as well as the fact that these prophecies did not deliver.

For example, the growth of science did not solve the crisis of the modern world as Comte expected, nor did the communist revolution usher in the benefits Marx predicted. In fact, we are all too familiar with the dark annals of the Communist experiment—especially in the area of human rights violation—and the uncertainty and meaninglessness spawned by modernism and postmodernism. Therefore we cannot ascribe credibility to either Marx or Comte. While their prophecies have failed, the eschatological vision of Seventh-day Adventists continues to be a source of hope and optimism to millions.

The foregoing discussions of the ways in which sociology can be specifically made to serve the Seventh-day Adventist world view is not, of course, limited to the selected doctrinal beliefs examined, nor are the examples given exhaustive. We can find other "good-fit" examples if we focus and commit ourselves to making every sociological idea, as far as possible, conducive to the glory of God.

References

Afanasyev, V. (1965). *Marxist philosophy: A popular outline.* Moscow: Progress.

Aron, R. (1968). *Main currents in sociological thought*, Vol. I. (R. Howard & H. Weaver, Trans.). New York: Anchor Books. (Original work published 1965)

Berger, P., & Luckman, T. (1966). *The social construction of reality.* New York: Doubleday.

Clark, R. A., & Gaede, S. D. (1987). Knowing together: Reflections on a holistic sociology of knowledge. In H. Heie & D. L. Wolfe (Eds.), *The reality of Christian learning: Strategies for faith-discipline integration* (pp. 55–86). Grand Rapids, MI: William B. Eerdmans.

Comte, A. (1855). *The positive philosophy* (H. Martineau, Trans.). New York: Calvin Blanchard.

Dulan, C. G. (1999). Teaching sociology: A biblical-Christian approach. In *Christ in the classroom: Adventist approaches to the integration of faith and learning* (Vol. 24, pp. 97–115). Compiled by H. M. Rasi. Silver Spring, MD: Institute for Christian Teaching.

Hobbes, T. (1909). *The Leviathan.* Oxford: Clarendon.

Journal of Research on Christian Education (JRCE), (2001). [Special Issue], 10.

Kelley, D. M. (1977). *Why conservative churches are growing* (2nd ed.). New York: Harper & Row.

Land, G. (2000). *Teaching history: A Seventh-day Adventist approach.* Berrien Springs, MI: Andrews University Press.

Marx, K., & Engels, F. (1960). *The German ideology.* New York: International Publishers.

Matthews, L. (1999). Dimensions of the integration of faith and learning: A sociological perspective. In *Christ in the classroom: Adventist approaches to the integration of faith and learning* (Vol. 24, pp. 177–196). Compiled by H. M. Rasi. Silver Spring, MD: Institute for Christian Teaching.

McBride, D. C. (1996). The sociological imagination and a Christian world view. In *Christ in the classroom: Adventist approaches to the integration of faith and learning* (Vol. 18, pp. 355–357). Complied by H. M. Rasi. Silver Spring, MD: Institute for Christian Teaching.

Roberts, K. A. (2000). *Religion in sociological perspective.* Belmont, CA: Thomson Learning Custom Publishing.

Seventh-day Adventists believe: A biblical exposition of 27 fundamental doctrines. (1988). Washington, DC: Ministerial Association, General Conference of Seventh-day Adventists.

Seventh-day Adventist Yearbook (2005). Hagerstown, MD: Review and Herald Publishing Association.

Thomas, W. I., & Znaniecki, F. (1918). *The Polish peasant in Europe and America.* Chicago: University of Chicago Press.

Tonnies, F. (1988). *Community and society,* with a new introduction by John Samples. New Brunswick, NJ: Transaction Books. (Original work, *Gemeinschaft and Gesellschaft,* published 1887)

Velesquez, M. (2002). *Philosophy: A text with readings* (8th ed.). Belmont, CA: Wadsworth.

CHAPTER SIX

POSTMODERNISM, ADVENTISM, AND THE CHALLENGE OF INTEGRATION

Postmodernism and its antecedents of pre-modernism and modernism are discussed. Postmodernism is presented as both a challenge and an "ally" to the Christian worldview. Specific postmodern themes are identified and discussed, and ways of making the Adventist faith perspective and practice more appealing to the postmodern mind are explored.

So far, we have exercised but passing interest in the phenomenon of postmodernism. Yet this phenomenon, anchored in its radical social construction of reality, has shifted the sociological pendulum to the extreme of cultural relativity. Unlike the positivist vision and law-discovery focus that marked the onset of sociology, the discipline now operates in an intellectual climate that opposes "notions of objectivity and scientific analysis" (Parrillo, 2002, p. 43). Thus, the modern outlook that informed the rise and development of sociology is being challenged and replaced by the postmodern mindset that rejects grand narratives. Also known as metanarratives, grand narratives are generally held belief systems that provide explanation and legitimation for broad cross-sections of social practices. Fragmentation and fluidity of standards and values became normative with the postmodern rejection of metanarratives. (See Table 6.1 for a comparison of modern/postmodern positions.)

Initially, sociologists reacted against a pre-modern mindset that regarded everything and every event in the world as being interconnected with every other, and ultimately enfolded in God. This pre-modern mindset viewed reality as "a rich tapestry of interwoven levels reaching from matter to body to mind to soul to spirit." It was a fused world, characterized by what Wilber refers to as "The Great Nest of Being" (Wilber, 1998, p. 6).

Needless to say, this integrated view of the world was substantially supplanted by the modern "flat land" view (Wilber, 1998, p. 7) that reduced everything to a material base. This scientific materialism worldview drew a sharp distinction between things that could be empirically validated and those that could not. Reality was thought to exist only in the sensory realm, and all else was but a figment of the imagination. Empirical science therefore became the ultimate standard for the study and validation of reality.

Table 6.1
Modernism and Postmodernism: A Contrast

Modernism	Postmodernism
Embraces the scientific method and seeks to understand objective evidence	Rejects objectivity. Suggests that we each develop in a context of local knowledge that shapes our worldview; that worldviews are little more than linguistic constructions; and that we reflect our particular time, place, and culture.
Accepts the assumptions of science: 1. the world is organized and structured by cause and effect 2. by studying the world scientifically, we can understand its essential balance and equilibrium	Sees the world as extremely complex and chaotic—a place where equilibrium has never and will never be achieved
Argues that society is rooted in the empirical, and that values will evolve toward an equilibrium in which individuals will find their proper place	Suggests that hierarchies of privilege and divisions by ethnicity will persist, that norms and values exist in social contexts and can only be judged or understood in those contexts, and that so-called objective scientific writings are to be understood by seeing how the author's social background led to their construction

Modernism	Postmodernism
Holds that nature is to be rationally exploited to create an environment for humans	Suggests that the environment has been used for greed in shortsighted over-development, that technology is now developing on a path of its own with little direction, that interest has put traditional nations and laws in jeopardy, and that current social arrangements are obsolete
Believes that intimacy and mutual support will be enhanced through progress, and that technology will allow more time for people to perfect their families and intimate arrangement	Points out three things: 1. post-industrial occupations have taken both parents out of the home 2. technology allows the simulation of intimacy as "real-time" intimacy 3. symbols, celebrities, and their images will replace "reality" and further develop mass consumerism as a way of life
Offers a master narrative of progress through science and technology	Points to skepticism of progress, anti-technology reactions, and new age religion
Creates a sense of a unified, centered self; "individualism"; and unified identity	Presents a picture of fragmentation and decentered self; multiple, conflicting identities
Sees "the family" as the central unit of social order and the middle-class, nuclear family as the model	Points out the new reality of alternative family units, alternatives to middle-class marriages, and multiple identities for couplings and child-raising
Sees hierarchy, order, and centralized control as structural assets	Presents subverted order and loss of centralized control fragmentation as the new reality
Maintains faith and personal investment in big politics (nation-state party)	Maintains trust and investment in micro-politics; identifies politics, local politics, institutional power struggles

Adapted from Parrillo (2002, p. 44)

Seventh-day Adventism, indeed all of Christianity in its Western manifestation, though reared in this climate of modernism, has always had a parallel, non-empirical, ultimate standard of its own. Hence, the challenge has always been to find points of convergence between disciplines such as sociology, which embraces the canon of scientific validation, and that of a faith perspective that does not appeal to such legitimation. But the challenge has never been insurmountable, notwithstanding the dichotomous nature of the base assumptions of the Christian and the scientific worldviews as they are conceived within the modernism project.

Though modernism, with its empiricist focus, de-emphasizes the non-empirical as a reality source, its embrace of an "out-there" objective reality makes it amenable to the Christian logic of a transcendent God, objective and independent of human construction. The Christian worldview and the modernist worldview thus seem joined, at least in their common acknowledgment of an objective reality (though this is only in the sensory realm for the latter). Thus, while the relationship between modernism and Christianity has been an uneasy one, there remains some basis for integration.

However, the challenge of integration appears less manageable in light of postmodern assumptions. Postmodernism not only does away with transcendent standards, but it denies that objective reality exists at all. Reality does not amount to anything more than what people make it out to be. It is local, provisional, and tentative. If indeed, following this logic, no ultimate point of reference exists, then not only religion but also the postmodern project itself is subverted, being no more or less valid than a mythic construction. Yet postmodernism, notwithstanding its non-commitment to objective truth, may be seized upon to facilitate discussions on the growing national, ethnic, and class diversity of Christianity, and in particular Seventh-day Adventism.

The postmodernist attributes equal worth to the varied ways in which people live. Not only does this legitimize cultural pluralism, but it also challenges Christians of different ethnic and social backgrounds to seek out ways to understand each other. This non-preferential posture of the postmodernist claim holds out promise for harmony in the face of the developing cosmopolitan nature of the Seventh-day Adventist church at a time when what it means to be Adventist is more fragmented than ever.

The cross-cultural contradictions posed by this growing diversity within the church may threaten frustration and disillusionment, but looking through the lens of the "impartial" postmodernist may ease the tension. Specifically, the spirit of compromise and tolerance may be indulged in order to facilitate dialogue and understanding. To be postmodern in this way does not translate to a temporary abandonment of biblical principles. Rather, it corresponds with the call to Christians (Seventh-day Adventists and non-Adventists alike) from different cultural backgrounds to be reflexive, that is, to find the humility to appreciate the viewpoint of the other. This willingness to grasp the peculiar reality of others from their standpoint coincides with the Pauline attitude and willingness "...to be...all things to all men...so that [he] may save some" (1 Cor. 9:19-23).

While adherence to this Pauline ethic of social sensitivity should deepen our corporate and individual capacities to appreciate and live peaceably with those of different cultural and value orientations, it also urges upon us the necessity to demonstrate the relevance of the church's world view and chosen lifestyle to the postmodern culture. The extent to which we are able to accomplish the latter will largely determine our ability to facilitate faith/discipline integration in the postmodern context.

The argument that Grenz (1996) makes regarding embedding the gospel in the postmodern situation seems applicable here. He suggests that the postmodern situation demands that the gospel be post-individualistic, post-rational, post-dualistic, and post-noeticentric (to be defined later). These emphases, he argues, can only make the gospel more understandable to the postmodern mind. Grenz's argument is rather compelling; if applied to the gospel in its Seventh-day Adventist manifestation, the gospel could be made much more relevant and acceptable to the current way of thinking. Although the identified themes resonate with the postmodern mindset, they are also deeply biblical. Let us examine each of them in turn.

Post-individualism

Post-individualism should not be taken to mean that people have lost their sense of individuality with the advent of postmodernism or that they should be encouraged to abandon such consciousness. Indeed, this would be contrary to biblical insight, for God has special regard for the individual (see John 3:16; Luke 15), and warns that every person must appear in the judgment to give account (Matt. 12:36). The point of emphasis here is upon the postmodernist's equal valuing of people and cultures, corresponding with Peter's dictum that "God is no respecter of persons" (Acts 10:35) and Paul's reminder that we are all children of God (Rom. 8:16).

While in the postmodernist position individuality per se is not ignored, the autonomous, superordinate, self-created individual is suspect. Hence, leaders who emphasize the power hierarchy at the expense of equality between themselves and their followers may soon have a waning impact on their followers. The history of trust betrayed in the idolization of the individual looms large in the examples of Hitler and Stalin, and more recently Jim Jones and David Koresh. The cult of the individual, or anything that is suggestive of it, is therefore not a positive image to the postmodern culture. If anything, this culture prefers the individual-in-community motif. Therefore, whatever removes the spotlight from the individual and promotes the communal should find easy acceptance with the postmodern mind. In the same way, wherever Seventh-day Adventism emphasizes the individual to the neglect of the community, it can only undermine its appeal to the current generation and thus hinder its chances of facilitating integration. This is true in the church's liturgical expressions, its general mode of operations, and the educational models it embraces.

Post-rationalism

Post-rationalism must also be understood in context. It does not suggest that Christians abandon reason in order to facilitate the integration of faith and learning. For God's demand that we exercise faith so that we may please Him (Heb. 11:6) is no less important than His invitation to us to reason with Him (Isa. 1:8). Seventh-day Adventism, as well as other forms of Christian expression, must recognize in their social practice that faith and reason are not necessarily antithetical entities.

Grenz's idea of post-rationalism stands in contrast to the variant of rational thought advocated by the Enlightenment thinkers. Such rationality is based ultimately on empirical logic, what Weber might call "Zweck-rationality," or rationality that emphasizes efficiency to the exclusion of other factors (see Perdue, 1986, p. 382). Habermas (1968) refers to it as "instrumental rationality" (p. 111) and argues that it is rooted in "technocratic consciousness," a form of consciousness that does not cater to the welfare of the whole. It easily surrenders the process to the outcome and fails to grasp the less obvious fact that "the ends are pre-existent in the means" (King, 1963, p. 95).

The Seventh-day Adventist school, for example, that draws on the insight of the post-rational ethic will therefore be integrated in its operation, balancing means and ends in ways that acknowledge the reciprocal relationship of the two. It will eschew the temptation of the success-at-any-cost philosophy, carefully selecting its method of operation, cognizant that the spirit and principle that characterize its chosen methods will be reproduced again in the behavioral and institutional outcomes generated. As Seventh-day Adventist schools seek to aid the wider church organization in the realization of its mission and goals in the postmodern world, this integrated policy approach will become increasingly necessary. While such an approach appeals to the postmodern mindset, it also draws on the wisdom of the principle implicit in Galatians 6:7, that the means are reproducible in the outcome (we reap what we sow). We cannot reap oats unless we sow oats. Similarly, corrupt means cannot but yield corrupt outcomes. Institutions that fail to recognize this principle in their operations are fated to gain reversals.

Post-dualism

The Cartesian mind-body dualism is at variance with biblical insights. In many ways, therefore, this philosophical position is rejected by the Seventh-day Adventist church in its embrace of a holistic view of humankind. Mind and body, like the body and the soul, are not distinctly separate entities; they are rather mutually inclusive aspects of the human person. Nowhere is this view better expressed than in the Seventh-day Adventist church's position on the state of the dead. Here the soul is not deemed to be separable from the body but is in fact a result of the joint interaction of spirit and body. Seventh-day Adventists teach that at death human consciousness ceases, since the breath of life (the spirit) needs the medium of the body for human consciousness to be possible (Eccl. 9:10; Gen. 2:7). This holistic view of life is traceable in other areas of the teachings of Seventh-day Adventism. For instance, Ellen White (1903) captures this theological position when she notes that the work of education and redemption are one, and that true education comprehends the harmonious development of the mental, physical, and spiritual faculties. Notwithstanding these examples, the day-to-day operations of the Seventh-day Adventist church sometimes display tendencies towards dualism.

One example of this is the sacred/secular differentiation made of its workers in determining how the tithe income is allocated. The work of pastors and Bible workers is deemed sacred and can be fully funded by the tithe, while the work of those who are engaged in the secular realm, such as social and natural scientists or teachers of the humanities, may not be so funded. This remains so whether these "others" are fully engaged in the various institutions of the church. Consequently, some have come to associate the call of God for service in the gospel ministry to mean only pastoral ministry or associated roles such as that of the Bible worker.

While the church needs to emphasize the distinction between the reality of God and the human/social reality, any of its practices that undermine the holistic nature of humans and the associated operational reality cannot but undermine the confidence and allegiance of the postmodern mind. Hence, wherever holism is emphasized in Seventh-day Adventism, this should be encouraged; positions that tend towards dualism, such as the dichotomy placed between the spiritual and the social, should be de-emphasized. John's view that we cannot truly love God while being at variance with our fellow humans (1 John 4:20) clues us into the mutually inclusive nature of the social and the spiritual. As has been previously suggested, this is the cornerstone point of the incarnation—God fulfilling Himself in the human context. Further, a spiritual/social dualism breeds hypocrisy in that it permits a disconnection between our love for God and our love for our fellow humans. This appears to be the basis upon which some people are able to exploit, dehumanize, and sometimes even kill others, while maintaining what they believe to be an intact relationship with God.

Post-noeticentricism

The root of the word "noeticentricism" lies in its Greek equivalent, *noetikas*, which means "intellectual." A noeticentric religion, therefore, is one that emphasizes the intellect to the exclusion of action; educational institutions are also highly liable to commit this sin. A post-noeticentric religion, on the other hand, seeks to match its embrace of knowledge with an action orientation. While it values knowledge, it avoids a fixation on mere empirical knowledge. While it aims at genuine praxis, matching theory with action, it reckons the indwelling of the Holy Spirit as a source of the knowledge base (theory) by which action is guided. It is truly Bible-based religion, known by its fruits (Matt. 7:20) and sustained by the Spirit (Rom. 8:14).

If the integration of faith and learning through sociology is to be effective in aiding the process of transformation in Jesus, it must transcend the conceptual level. In this regard, the most potent factor of faith/discipline integration is the sociology teacher and student themselves. What is missing is not so much theories and conceptual models as real life examples. Integrated teachers and students, those whose lives embody the very Bible-based principles they wish to convey and amplify through their teaching and scholarship, provide the most compelling witness of the possibility of faith/discipline integration.

References

Grenz, S. J. (1996). *A primer on postmodernism.* Grand Rapids, MI: Wm. B. Eerdmans Publishing Co.

Habermas, J. (1968). *Toward a rational society.* Boston: Beacon Press.

King, M. L., Jr. (1963). *Strength to love.* New York: Harper & Row.

Parrillo, V. N. (2002). *Contemporary social problems* (5th ed.). Boston: Allyn and Bacon.

Perdue, W. D. (1986). Sociological theory: Explanation, paradigm, and ideology. Palo Alto, CA: Mayfield Publishing Company.

White, E. G. (1903). *Education.* Hagerstown, MD: Review and Herald Publishing Association.

Wilber, K. (1998). *The marriage of sense and soul: Integrating science and religion.* New York: Random House.

RECOMMENDED READING

Baum, G. (1975). *Religion and alienation: A theological reading of sociology*. New York: Paulist Press. The rich and provocative insights of a Catholic priest's encounter with the sociology of religion are offered in this book.

Berger, P. (1961). *The noise of solemn assemblies*. Garden City, NY: Doubleday & Co. A popular treatment of Christian commitment, this book is about the religious establishment in America.

Berger, P., & Luckman, T. (1967). *The social construction of reality: A treatise in the sociological of knowledge*. Garden City, NY: Doubleday & Co. This is Berger's major synthesis of the sociology of knowledge.

Berger, P., & Pullberg, S. (1965). Reification and the sociological critique of consciousness. *History and Theory, 4,* 196–201. The authors produced a technical but illuminating study in a specialized area of the sociology of knowledge.

Blackburn, J. (1972). *The earth is the Lord's?* Waco, TX: Word. A Christian writer describes how the threat to the Georgia tideland marshes near her home awakened her to ecological issues. She discovered that strategic efforts by informed citizens can be politically effective. This is an interesting account and useful handbook for individuals, church groups, and faith-at-work organizations who are seeking to actively relate the Christian perspective in ecology to political decision makers.

Campolo, A. (1983). *The power delusion*. Wheaton, IL: Victor Books. Written in Campolo's engaging style, this is a useful and provocative critique of power for the Christian.

Christians, C. G., & Van Hook, J. M. (Eds.). (1981). *Jacques Ellul: Interpretive essays*. Urbana, IL: University of Illinois Press. A valuable collection of essays by Christian commentators of Ellul's work.

Costas, O. E. (1974). *The church and its mission: A shattering critique from the third world*. Wheaton, IL: Tyndale. A penetrating account of the factors associated with the alleged failure of the church in the third world.

Demant, V. A. (1963). *Christian sex ethics*. New York: Harper and Row. A professor at Oxford and Anglican canon of Christ's Church sensitively

speaks to the many issues raised by the sexual revolution of the six-
ties. He speaks of chastity, eroticism, gender differences, meaning of
marriage, cohabiting, and many other current issues from historical,
ethical, and biblical standpoints.

DeSanto, C. P., Redekop, C., & Smith-Hinds, W. L. (1980). *A reader in
sociology: Christian perspectives.* Scottdale, PA: Herald Press. A useful and reliable collection of essays that meets the needs of both the
lay person and the scholar.

Ellul, J. (1967). *The presence of the kingdom.* New York: Seabury Press.
The place to begin a study of Ellul's work is here. It is highly recommended reading for the Christian.

Ellul, J. (1969). *Violence.* New York: Seabury Press. This is a provocative
and very readable segment of Ellul's work.

Ellul, J. (1970). *The meaning of the city.* Grand Rapids, MI: Wm. B.
Eerdmans. This well-known biblical analysis of the city presents the
dialectical nature of reality as conceived by Ellul.

Ellul, J. (1984). *Money and power.* Downers Grove, IL: InterVarsity Press.
A well-written and penetrating critique and analysis of social issues
Christians will find helpful.

Ellwood, C. (1922). *The reconstruction of religion: A sociological view.*
New York: Macmillan & Co. This is one of the important statements
on the Social Gospel by a prominent sociologist of the day.

Engstrom, T. W. (1976). *The making of a Christian leader.* Grand Rapids,
MI: Zondervan.

Engstrom, T. W., & Dayton, E. R. (1976). *The art of management for Christian leaders.* Waco, TX: Word Books. These two books by Engstrom
are cited as examples of an approach to organization and leadership
that tends to be in contrast with the institutional philosophy set out in
this essay. Engstrom tends toward the technical organizational model,
although some consideration is given to a team approach in the latter
volume.

Evans, C. S. (1977). *Preserving the person.* Downers Grove, IL: InterVarsity
Press. Written by an evangelical Christian philosopher, this is a useful
critique of the human sciences.

Folsom, P. (1971). *And thou shalt die in a polluted land: An approach to
Christian ecology.* Liguori, MO: Liguorian Pamphlets and Books.
This one-hundred-page paperback was written by a Catholic priest. It

raises many issues for those who seek to examine the Bible, faith, and responsibility in ecology from a Christian perspective.

Gaede, S. D. (1985). *Belonging.* Grand Rapids, MI: Zondervan Publishing Co. Represents a contemporary Christian statement on the importance of community in church and family.

Gangel, K. O. (1977). Toward a biblical theology of marriage and family. *Journal of Psychology and Theology 1,* 55-69; *2,* 150-162; *3,* 247-259; *4,* 318-351. An excellent four-part series outlining in some detail the roles and responsibilities of Christians within the family, the roles of the family as a social structure, relationships within the family structure, and issues and problems relating to parenting. The influences of culture are considered.

Grunlan, S. A., & Mayers, M. K. (1979). *Cultural anthropology: A Christian perspective.* Grand Rapids, MI: Zondervan. A basic introduction to cultural anthropology that provides a background for understanding the nature and dynamics of culture.

Guinness, O. (1983). *The Gravedigger files.* Downers Grove, IL: InterVarsity Press. Witty and sophisticated, this book offers the Christian a rich introduction to the sociology of knowledge and the foibles of the church.

Harris, R. A. (2004). *The integration of faith and learning: A world view approach.* Eugene, OR: Cascade Books. An excellent exposition of the faith-learning integration construct. A must read.

Hirschi, T. (1969). *Causes of delinquency.* Berkeley, CA: University of California Press. Probably the most comprehensive presentation and empirical evaluation of the social control theory. Contrasts the basic tenets of several major deviance perspectives.

Holmes, A. (1977). *All truth is God's truth.* Grand Rapids, MI: Wm. B. Eerdmans Publishing Co. This book is a lucid and well-reasoned statement of some of the theological and philosophical arguments concerning the nature of truth.

Hopkins, C. H. (1940). *The rise of the social gospel in American Protestantism: 1865-1915.* New Haven, CT: Yale University Press. Here is the definitive work on the topic.

Jeeves, M. A. (1969). *The scientific enterprise and Christian faith.* Downers Grove, IL: InterVarsity. A book based on a conference in which thirty-six scientists discussed the relationship between science and the

Christian faith. The book develops a biblical view of the relationship of God to His creation and explains some of the key concepts in modern science and their relationship to Christian beliefs.

Johnson, A. (1976). History and culture in New Testament interpretation. In S. J. Schultz and M. A. Inch (Eds.), *Interpreting the Word of God.* Chicago: Moody Press. An excellent discussion of the importance of interpreting Scripture in the light of its cultural context. Discusses issues and gives examples.

Kilinski, K. K., & Wofford, J. C. (1973). *Organization and leadership in the local church.* Grand Rapids, MI: Zondervan. An excellent example of the application of the "body concept" to the organization of the local church. Outlines the application of leadership principles consistent with biblical objectives.

Kuhn, T. S. (1962). *The structure of scientific revolutions.* Chicago: University of Chicago Press. A useful discussion of the scientific enterprise and its pre-theoretical aspect.

Lovelace, R. (1979). *The dynamics of spiritual life.* Downers Grove, IL: InterVarsity Press. Although not exclusively devoted to the small group, this book conveys the role and impact the small group could and should have in church renewal.

Lyon, D. (1975). *Christians and sociology.* Downers Grove, IL: InterVarsity Press. Lyon's brief book is a good place for Christians to begin a study of the subject.

Mayers, M. K. (1974). *Christianity confronts culture.* Grand Rapids: Zondervan. An excellent approach to cross-cultural communication of the gospel. Deals with the issue of biblical authority and cultural relativity and applies it to contemporary situations.

Meier, P. D. (1977). *Christian child-rearing and personality development.* Grand Rapids, MI: Baker Book House. Meier, a physician and a psychiatrist who teaches at Dallas Theological Seminary, here provides a longitudinal presentation of principles related to personality and socialization. It is not a technical book, but offers a practical approach to the application of biblical and scientific principles.

Mills, T. M. (1967). *The sociology of small groups.* Englewood Cliffs, NJ: Prentice-Hall. Excellent introduction to the area from the classic social system perspective.

Moberg, D. (1962, June). Cultural relativity and Christian faith. *Journal of the American Scientific Affiliation, 14*(2), 34–48. Moberg makes a statement on culture that is important for all Christians.

Moberg, D. (1970, March). The manipulation of human behavior. *Journal of the American Scientific Affiliation, 22*(1), 14–17. Here is an insightful analysis of the problem for the Christian.

Moberg, D. (1985). *Wholistic Christianity: An appeal for a dynamic, balanced faith.* Elgin, IL: Brethren Press. This is an insightful critique of contemporary American Protestantism.

Myers, D. G. (1978). *The human puzzle: Psychological research and Christian belief.* New York: Harper & Row. The subtitle of this book summarizes its theme. It is an excellent commentary on the assumptions of research and their biblical implications. No Christian student of the social sciences should proceed without reading this book.

Nida, E. (1954). *Customs and cultures.* New York: Harper. Written by a Christian anthropologist, this book offers an early and clear defense for the application of anthropology to missions.

Niebuhr, H. R. (1951). *Christ and culture.* New York: Harper & Row. This is a classic and influential statement of a Christian view of culture.

Niebuhr, H. R. (1957). *The social sources of denominationalism.* New York: Median Books. This is an important account of the social forces that inform the differences among denominations. An excellent read for those who are pursuing an understanding of the sociological connection of the church.

Perkins, R. (1987). *Looking both ways.* Grand Rapids, MI: Baker Book House. This is a well-reasoned and lucid defense of the sociology of knowledge.

Poloma, M. M. (1979). *Contemporary sociological theory.* New York: Macmillan Publishing Co. Written by a Christian, this is a well-designed and readable source for the lay person.

Redekop, C. (1970). *The free church and seductive culture.* Scottdale, PA: Herald. Although primarily a discussion of the Free Church tradition and organization, there are several excellent chapters on the problems of human relationships and how the Christian is to relate to others through his or her statuses.

Rushdoony, R. J. (1976). *Intellectual schizophrenia.* Phillipsburg, NJ: Presbyterian and Reformed. An examination of the philosophical implications of secularized education, with a Christian perspective. This book will cause you to think. Although not primarily a volume about socialization, the first chapter is entitled "The School and the Whole Person," giving evidence of Rushdoony's understanding that schooling plays a large part in forming the personality.

Schaeffer, F. A. (1978). *The church at the end of the 20th century.* Downers Grove, IL: InterVarsity Press. This book brings into sharp focus the need to militantly preserve the traditional biblical mission of the church. A forceful demonstration of the attrition of Christian values.

Schaeffer, F. A., & Koop, C. E. (1979). *Whatever happened to the human race?* Old Tappan, NJ: Revell. A forceful presentation of the dehumanizing trends in society by two renowned authorities in their field. Schaeffer, a Christian philosopher, and Koop, surgeon-in-chief of Philadelphia's Children's Hospital, address such topics as abortion, euthanasia, and infanticide from a biblical perspective. This book, along with the film series that accompanies it, is strongly recommended to the student.

Small, D. H. (1959). *Design for Christian marriage.* Westwood, NJ: Revell. An older book that has had very wide usefulness in colleges, churches, and homes. Rich in scriptural interpretation, allusions to literature, and utilization of social science, it succeeds in integrating them in an interesting and helping way. This book should be in every person's library. Chapter Four on "Sex as Symbol and Sacrament" is an especially good correction to distorted views about sex found both in the church and secular society.

Stevenson, L. (1974). *Seven theories on human nature.* New York: Oxford University Press. A short but thought-provoking book that summarizes, compares, and contrasts seven perspectives on understanding the nature of the universe and humanity, and also the human predicament and its solution. The Christian perspective is included, stimulating further development of the political implications of such a perspective.

Stott, J. R. W. (1978). *Christian counter culture: The message of the sermon on the mount.* Downers Grove, IL: InterVarsity Press. The title could be deceiving. This is a commentary on the Sermon on the Mount written in Stott's lucid and anecdotal style.

The Willowbank Report—Gospel and Culture. Wheaton, IL: Lausanne Committee for World Evangelization, 1978. A report of the consultation on the gospel and culture held at Willowbank, Bermuda, in January 1978. A good discussion of contextualization and cross-cultural ministry.

Tweedell, C. (2004). *Sociology: A Christian approach for changing the world.* Marion, IN: Triangle Publishing. This book is one of the few principles of sociology texts with a distinct Christian perspective.

Van Til, H. R. (1959). *The Calvinistic concept of culture.* Grand Rapids, MI: Baker Book House. Though theologically biased, this is a rich work on the subject of culture and free will.

Walsh, B. J., & Middleton, J. R. (1984). *The transforming vision: Shaping a Christian world view.* Downers Grove, IL: InterVarsity Press. A useful book covering a number of topics integral to the faith-learning construct. A must read.

Walter, J. A. (1979). *Sacred cows: Exploring contemporary idolatry.* Grand Rapids, MI: Zondervan Publishing Co. With a lucid and probing style, Walter exposes some rarely identified idols for the Christian.

Webber, R. E. (1979). *The secular saint.* Grand Rapids, MI: Zondervan Publishing Co. An interesting treatment of Christian social responsibility from an evangelical perspective. Webber discusses and critiques three models found in evangelical circles.

Weber, M. (1930). *The Protestant ethic and the spirit of capitalism.* New York: Charles Scribner's Sons. This is a classic on social thought.

USEFUL WEB SITES

Apologetics

Academy of Christian Apologetics
www.hisdefense.org/home2.html

Apologetics.com
www.apologetics.com

Apologetics.org
www.apologetics.org

Apologetics Index
www.apologeticsindex.org

Apologetics Information Ministries
www.apologeticsinfo.org

Atlanta Christian Apologetics
www.atlantaapologist.org

Center for Reformed Theology and Apologetics
www.reformed.org

Christian Answers Net
www.christiananswers.net

Christian Apologetics and Research Ministry
www.carm.org

Reasons to Believe
www.reasons.org

General Worldview Resources
Christian Leadership Ministries
www.clm.org

Doorway Papers
www.custance.org

The Integration of Faith and Learning
www.virtualsalt.com/int/

Internet Christian Library
www.iclnet.org

Leadership University
www.leaderu.com

Xenos Christian Fellowship
www.xenos.org

Periodicals
Books and Culture Magazine
www.christianitytoday.com/books/

BreakPoint Online
www.breakpoint.org

Christianity Today
www.christianitytoday.com

First Things
www.firstthings.com

World
www.worldmag.com

Science

Access Research Network
www.arn.org

Answers in Genesis
www.answeringenesis.org

Center for Science and Culture
www.discovery.org/crsc/

Origins.org
www.origins.org

THE INSTITUTE FOR CHRISTIAN TEACHING

The Institute for Christian Teaching (ICT) was established in 1987, through the generous donation of a Seventh-day Adventist businessman, to promote excellence in Adventist education. Under the direction of an Advisory Committee and the supervision of the Education Department of the General Conference of Seventh-day Adventists, the Institute offers seminars and develops resources to foster the integration of faith and learning in Christian schools, colleges, and universities.

Since 1988 and with additional funding from the General Conference of Seventh-day Adventists and other donors, the Institute has sponsored international faith and learning seminars for educators in the United States as well as in Argentina, Australia, Bolivia, Brazil, Colombia, Côte d'Ivoire, England, France, Germany, India, Jamaica, Kenya, Korea, Mexico, Nigeria, Peru, Philippines, Singapore, South Africa, and Thailand.

The Institute for Christian Teaching pursues the following objectives:

1. To promote excellence—professional and spiritual—in Seventh-day Adventist teaching at the secondary and post-secondary levels.
2. To foster the integration of faith and learning throughout the curriculum on the basis of a comprehensive Christian worldview.
3. To focus on the uniqueness, values, and implications of Seventh-day Adventist educational philosophy.
4. To stimulate research and publication in the area of Christ-centered, Bible-based, and service-oriented education.

At present, the Institute has published more than 600 monographs on secondary, college/university, and professional topics, developed by participants in the faith and learning seminars. These can be obtained individually or in bound volumes in the *Christ in the Classroom* series. Some of these essays can be downloaded from our website, listed below.

For a free catalogue of the materials available and information on upcoming seminars, contact:

The Institute for Christian Teaching
General Conference Education Department
12501 Old Columbia Pike
Silver Spring, MD 20904-6600, U.S.A.
Telephone: (301) 680-5060
Fax: (301) 622-9627
Website: http://ict.adventist.org
E-mail: rodrigueze@gc.adventist.org

THE CENTER FOR COLLEGE FAITH

The Center for College Faith is an initiative of Andrews University which seeks to help faculty better understand and foster the faith development of college undergraduates. Membership in the Center is open to all Andrews University faculty and is voluntary. The Center was formally organized in 1998, but its origin lies in a faculty convocation in 1996 which recognized a need to more effectively highlight faith development as central to the entire undergraduate experience.

The stated mission of the Center is twofold. First, we seek to acquire and disseminate knowledge about how college students develop in their Christian beliefs, values, and lifelong commitment to God, especially in relation to direct academic experiences. Second, we endeavor to promote on the Andrews University campus the growth of a distinctly Christian undergraduate "culture of learning" informed by careful scholarship.

Funded by generous donors, the Center has co-sponsored (with the Institute for Christian Teaching) the Faith and Learning Conference at Andrews University in 1999 and the publication of the Faith and Learning Series of which the present volume is the third. Center activities include an active research initiative focused on the college impact on spiritual formation of undergraduates; a development program for Center faculty which supports professional growth, scholarship, and curricular revision pertinent to the Center's mission; a faculty seminar series to promote dialogue on issues of faith development; and the support for publishing scholarship at the interface of Christian faith and the Academy.

For further information, please contact the director of the Center:

Mickey D. Kutzner
Physics Department
Andrews University
Berrien Springs, MI 49104
(269) 471-6291
kutzner@andrews.edu

INDEX

A
Absolute God 33, 34
Absolute truth 34, 35
Absolutism 33, 54
Anomalies 56, 57

B
Babylon 50, 52
Bates, Joseph 59
Berger, Peter 32
Biography 5
Blumer, Herbert G. 31, 41, 51, 64, 69, 85
Bureaucracy 51, 54, 73

C
Campolo, Tony 47
Capitalism 21, 22, 101, 121
Cartesian block 46
Christian Connexion 50
Christianity, assumptions of 23
Christian worldview 13, 17, 22, 23, 25, 27, 28, 30-34, 36, 69, 71, 80, 81, 83, 105, 108
Church, life cycle of 45, 51
Class-derived knowledge 33
Class conflict 21, 22, 101
Co-creators 77
Collectivist assumption 18
Communal 13, 98, 110
Communicated ideas 80
Communitarian beliefs 96
Compatibalist integration 71
Complete disjunction 68
Comte, Auguste 20-22, 25, 27, 28, 41, 101, 102
Conflict perspective vii, 23-25, 27, 41
Conjunction vii, 68
Connexionist 50
Constructionism 17, 21, 22, 34
Cooley, Charles Horton 11, 13
Correlation integration 68
Cosmos ix, 72
Cross-cultural 108, 118, 120
Cult of the individual 110
Cultural pluralism 108
Cultural relativity 33, 34, 36, 42, 105, 118

D
Deliberate integration 69
Determinable creatures 36
Determinism 17, 22, 28, 62
Dialogical integration 69
Dichotomous 45, 63, 76-78, 108
   subject/object construct 77
Disintegration 51, 53, 54, 56
Diversity 14, 56, 108
Divine accommodation 45, 46, 66
Divine intervention ix, 45, 62, 63
Dualism 46, 62, 111, 112
   post-dualism 111
   spiritual/social 112
Dudley, Roger 48, 49, 64
Durkheim, Emile 3, 10, 13, 21, 22, 29, 42, 98

E
Economists 3
Empirical rationality 67

Empirical science 22, 75, 101, 106
Empiricist 22, 36, 39, 47, 76, 108
Enlightenment 18-21, 25, 29, 67, 110
Epistemology 23, 42
Eschatological vision 25, 100, 102
Evangelical movement 68
Externalization 32
Extra-individual 28, 93

F

Faith-based perspective 90
Faith/learning integration ix, 67-71,
     76, 80, 83, 85, 91
False consciousness 21, 31, 46
Formal organization 49-53, 73
Fraser, David A. 47
Free-will 81, 92
French Revolution 18, 20, 21, 25
Fundamentalists 67, 68
Fusion integration 68

G

General Conference vi-viii, x, 52, 54,
     58, 59, 64, 91, 103
Genie 11, 12
God-man 63
God as a group 12
Grand narratives 105
Grenz, Stanley 7, 14, 109, 110, 113
Group dynamics 97, 99
Groupness 2, 12, 92
Guy, Fritz 59, 60, 64, 65

H

Heddendorf, Russell 7, 9, 14
Hernandez, Edwin 48, 49, 64
History vi, 5, 24, 47, 51, 52, 54, 56,
     60, 85, 103, 110, 115, 118
Holism 46, 112

Holistic 2, 41, 46, 47, 61, 63, 64, 70,
     96, 98, 102, 111, 112
Holistic approach 70, 98
Holistic development 2, 46
Holmes, Arthur F. 68, 86, 117
Holy Spirit 52, 59, 91, 94, 98, 99, 112
Human/divine relationship 77
Humanism 17, 22, 24, 43
     in symbolic interactionism 31
Humanistic sociology 29-31, 36
     assumptions of 29

I

Ideal factors 33
Idealists 47
Image of God 4, 6, 78, 92-94
Incarnation 45, 46, 63, 70, 112
Incipient organization 51, 53
Incorporation integration 68
Individual-in-community motif 110
Individualistic fallacy 9, 10
Injunction 68
Institutionalism 51, 54, 65
Institution building 67, 80-83
Instrumental rationality 110
Integrating biblical concepts 72
Interactionist perspective vii, 69, 70,
     94
Internalization 32, 61
Interpersonal 3, 97
Intrapersonal 3
Iron law of oligarchy 51

J

Jehovah's Witnesses 48

K

Knight, George R. 48-52, 54, 55,
     59, 65

Y

Yinger, J. Milton 61, 66

Z

Zeitlin, Irving M. 19, 21, 30, 43